START YOUR OWN SANDWICH VAN BUSINESS

A cheaper alternative to a sandwich shop or coffee bar

OR

How to make a living selling sandwiches and other food from a mobile vehicle

Andrew Johnson

Castleriver Publishing
Hertfordshire, United Kingdom

D0488974

CRi

Castleriver Real World
An imprint of Castleriver Publishing

Published by Castleriver Publishing

A catalogue record for this book is available from the British Library.

Cover design: Peter Henderson
Composition: Helen Robbins
Series design: Pam Edwards

About the author

After nearly fourteen years spent repairing and installing IT equipment, Andrew Johnson gave up the day job and started his own business. Dabbling with ideas as diverse as picture framing and tyre fitting, he eventually decided to buy a van and start a sandwich round. Two shops and three sandwich vans later, he has written this book to guide anyone else thinking of following the same path.

If you're thinking about starting your own mobile sandwich delivery business then the information contained in this book could be invaluable. This is one author who doesn't skimp on the detail.

CRi
Castleriver Publishing

Regulations regarding environmental health are updated from time to time. For the most current information, please contact your local authority either by phoning or visiting their website.

The information contained in this book has been assembled with care. No responsibility for loss or injury can be accepted by the author or publisher as a result of action or inaction taken based upon material contained within this publication.

Contents

Preface

About this book

I have been involved in the sandwich trade for a long time now, and I have seen the business from both sides of the fence, first with sandwich rounds, and then with shops.

I aim to share my experiences, good and bad, with the intention of making your journey easier, hopefully showing you the advantages of starting a sandwich round in preference to another business type.

A good living

My own expertise comes from owning two sandwich shops and operating three sandwich vans. I have earned a good living, but I am not a millionaire just yet, and I am not claiming that you will make a million running a sandwich round either.

I do believe that if you have the determination and the right mindset, you can make a very comfortable living and have fun (most days!) in this business.

That's not to say you can't build up an empire from running a sandwich round. A lot of famous people started small, but didn't stay that way. You may start with a sandwich round and go on to open a full retail shop, and establish an empire, or perhaps buy more sandwich vans and develop more sandwich rounds.

No padding

There are two aspects to starting a business. The general commercial side that applies to all new ventures, such as creating a business plan, finding an accountant and raising finance. And the second part that is specific to the particular business you are starting.

This book concerns the specifics of starting a sandwich round business using a sandwich van. The only references to bookkeeping, accountants or tax law that you will see are where those matters directly apply to the business itself. For example hygiene law is covered because it's specific to the food industry.

You won't find 50 pages on writing a business plan, or finding a lawyer. There are umpteen books on Amazon concerning general business start ups. It is not my intention to clog up or pad out the book on those general issues. In the following pages, you will find the gritty detail of starting or buying a sandwich round.

Chapter One

The Sandwich Trade Revealed

Before getting into the details of why a sandwich round is a good choice of business compared to a sandwich shop or, for that matter, compared to most other business types, it's worth spending a few minutes defining just what a sandwich round is.

Definition of a Sandwich Round

A sandwich round is generally defined as a van that calls at businesses on a daily basis, at set times and usually at the same spot.

A sandwich van will often carry much more than just sandwiches. Quite often the range will include hot food such as pies and sausages, as well as crisps, cakes, drinks, yoghurts and any other snacks that the owner sees a demand for.

The type of vehicle can vary from the simplest of panel vans, costing a few thousand pounds, right through to a professional Jiffy Truck that could lighten your wallet by £25,000 or more.

The Outlook for a Sandwich Based Business

As I write this, in the closing days of September 2008, the economic outlook seems bleak – not much good news on the business front. Despite this, there are several reasons why starting a sandwich round, in preference to most other business types, makes sense.

The market is huge and getting bigger

The number of sandwiches purchased in the UK every year is about 2,500 million – add this to the number we make at home and the figure exceeds 12 billion!

We munch our way through more sandwich than any other kind of food, and that includes burgers, chips, Chicken Tikka Masalas and even crisps. Nothing comes close to the popularity of the sandwich; it is truly the Emperor of daytime foods.

The competition is flagging

Something else to consider. The sandwich market is the fastest growing sector of the food retailing industry. Whilst sales of burgers and fried chicken are falling, sandwiches are just getting more popular.

The main reasons are health related. A sandwich is seen as a healthier option to traditional fast foods such as burgers or fried chicken and there is no reason to believe that this perception will lesson in the future.

Job security

It's a cliché to say (but still true) that people have to eat. A sandwich is seen as a modest purchase, one that can be made even when times are tough. However, in financially difficult times, luxury food spending such as a restaurant visit is usually cut down.

You could never describe any business as recession proof, but a quality sandwich based business is probably as close as you could get.

It's Not Just the Money

There are plenty of reasons, other than financial, to start a sandwich round as opposed to another business type.

Expandable business

A sandwich van can do much more than sell sandwiches to the lunchtime trade. You are free to experiment with bagels, wraps, baked goods, organic foods, fresh fruit etc.

You can add to, or change the menu at the drop of a hat. You could aim to develop a breakfast trade, tempting hungry workers with coffee and croissants on the way to the office, or perhaps target shift workers in the early evening.

That's not the half of it, future expansion could involve you in outside catering, or even special event catering.

The point I am trying to make here, is that few businesses can be expanded, refocused or reinvented beyond the original concept, with such ease. It's a useful advantage.

A cash business that you can run from home

Your work is done from your van, apart from admin tasks, which can be done at home. There are situations where you can make sandwiches at home and sell them in the van. Or even easier, buy the sandwiches in from a supplier. The vast majority of your sales will be cash based, with no credit card accounts to worry about.

Pleasant working hours

Most sandwich vans head home after about 3pm. That's a nice early finish that allows you to get lots of other business related tasks completed and be finished working at a respectable hour.

A clean business

A sandwich round is a very clean business, even if you sell hot food, it won't be fried food, but rather pies, sausages or jacket potatoes. Compare that to a fish and chip shop, where the cooking odours can become overpowering.

Why a Sandwich Round and not a Retail Shop?

Any choice of business will be decided upon by a mixture of personal preferences and circumstances – the most obvious being the availability of capital.

Having been involved in both types, I feel I am qualified to offer my observations and outline the advantages and disadvantages of choosing to start a sandwich round instead of opening a sandwich shop.

Some of the points listed below will be examined in more detail in later chapters, as there is a large degree of crossover between the two business types.

Start up costs are lower and start up times are quicker

The costs of establishing a retail sandwich shop can be considerable, a figure of £90,000 would not be excessive, and that is by no means the ceiling.

A sandwich round can be started for little more than the cost of a suitable van (new or used) and some working capital. Starting a retail shop, with all the complexities and potential problems that involves, can take nearly a year. A sandwich round could be up and running within months.

Flexible working location

If one area is not producing sales, you can drive to another one. If you have a shop and sales fall off, you can't uproot it and move somewhere else.

Much simpler business type

There are no landlords, mortgages, or building repairs to worry about. Granted, you might have a lease vehicle for a sandwich round, but upkeep on a van is a lot less hassle than maintaining a commercial building.

Easier to carry out market research

I will examine market research in detail in a later chapter, but for now, just accept that the process is cheaper and far easier for a sandwich round business, than for a fixed retail shop.

Staffing issues

Generally, you won't have any because you are the staff! A sandwich shop always needs more than one staff member, even if they are part time. This brings a new level of complexity and legal obligation to the business.

More variety

A van can't easily compete in terms of variety of products, but many vans sell hot food such as pies or sausages, and most sandwich shops are not licensed to sell hot food – a sandwich van can make a lot of extra money selling hot food.

It's Not All a Bed of Roses

There are a few disadvantages to starting a sandwich round when compared to a retail sandwich shop, and these, in my view, are the major ones.

The competition can be fierce

Knowing the competition is vital before you even start the business, I cover that in the section on market research. But even if you know the competition at the start, it's easy for new vans to invade your patch, and you need techniques to make sure you stay in the lead – I provide techniques and tips later in the book.

Vans can break down

Probably the single biggest fear of a sandwich round business owner is a breakdown. It can happen, but it's not common. If you keep your vehicle in good order and service it regularly you won't have many problems. Believe me, you won't lose your customers if your van is out of action for a day or two.

Building business can be slow

It's a sad fact that sandwich vans have not always enjoyed a glorious reputation – in fact a decade ago they were often seen as cowboy operators with dubious hygiene standards. Thankfully that is changing, but be prepared for a slow build up whilst people get to know you.

Lack of a business base

It can be hard to feel attached to a business without a fixed location, your workplace will be a mobile van.

The State of the UK Sandwich Market

With an annual turnover approaching £3.5 billion, the value of the sandwich market is huge. But even though the public are buying more sandwiches than ever, their expectations have changed quite dramatically over the past 15 years.

Once upon a time, two slices of white bread, smeared with margarine and finished off with plain Cheddar would have been the norm for a typical cheese sandwich, and if you were really lucky, it was less than a week old. Alright, that is a bit of an exaggeration, but not much.

Changing tastes

Nowadays, if you tried to offer that from your sandwich van, as a staple sandwich, you wouldn't get much business. The public's perception of what constitutes a good sandwich has changed dramatically. Tastes have become much more adventurous and exotic – and your menu must reflect that.

Fillings such as Cajun Chicken, Crayfish and Rocket, Thai Prawn and Mayonnaise, and plenty more, may be on your menu to cater for more sophisticated palettes. A modern sandwich van must be prepared to stock the sandwiches that appeal to the client base – if you don't, your competitors will. That's not to say that you won't be stocking all the old favourites, such as the BLT or Chicken and Mayonnaise, you certainly will, because they sell well.

You will see that I have included a lot of information in later chapters about sandwich breads as well. A lot of sandwich vans still don't offer a good range of bread, if yours does, that could be the edge that gets you the customers – and keeps them

Time challenged workers

Modern working life doesn't leave a lot of time for preparing food at home. Even making a sandwich takes time, and can be a hassle.

Picture the scene

Fifteen minutes before you leave for work, enough time to prepare a quick sandwich. Get the bread out, rummage in the fridge for the butter, and a tomato or two, look for your prize Red Leicester, oh dear, no cheese ? Some kind soul's eaten the lot? Put the butter back, reseal the bread bag ...

Far easier to pop out at lunch time and grab a bite to eat, and the sandwich you buy will be more interesting than the plain cheese and tomato you had in mind anyway.

This leads us nicely on to the next point. The sandwiches that a specialist van can offer will be more interesting and exotic than the average person can be bothered to make at home. Just as importantly, most consumers can afford the cost of a sandwich, it's a relatively painless purchase.

It's also highly likely that they will buy something else to go with their sandwich, a drink or a packet of crisps for example. In my experience, most of the time the purchaser buys more than just a sandwich.

Chapter Two

Sandwich Round Research

Planning a business without doing the groundwork is just asking for trouble. It's vital that you carry out research before committing to the project.

Unless the initial idea is sound, you face the very real prospect of wasting both time and money on a pointless venture. Your investigations will fall into two camps.

- Assessing your suitability to run a sandwich round.
- The viability of the actual business.

Let's start with the fundamental factor that will most affect the future of the potential business, namely, you.

Does the Sandwich Trade Suit You?

The idea of going into business for yourself sounds glamorous, but there are some serious points to consider before deciding whether it's right for you. It's easy to gloss over the potential problems, and get caught up in the excitement of the adventure.

Let me state right now that running a sandwich round is hard work, physically, mentally and emotionally.

Physical Demands

It's true that a lot of time is spent driving around and that doesn't sound so bad. But each place you visit means getting out of the van and serving your customers – doing this from 7.30 am in the morning to 3pm can be draining.

Also, there is a lot more to running a sandwich round than just driving the van and selling the stock. Purchasing stock can be very tiring, with a fair bit of lifting involved.

Some of the more physical activities might include:

- Preparing and loading the van. A fair bit of stretching and bending down is involved. If you suffer from a bad back, you will feel the strain.

- A lot of time spent sitting down. Again, if you suffer from back problems, how badly will you be affected by spending hours every day sitting in the driver's seat?

- Visiting your suppliers will mean some lifting, a lot of your stock will be purchased in bulk – for example, cartons of cold drinks are heavy.

- If you choose to make the sandwiches you sell, rather than buying them in, be prepared for lots of washing, chopping and generally preparing ingredients – usually standing up.

- Keeping the van clean and properly serviced. Unless you pay someone to do this for you, you will be washing the van yourself. In my experience, a sandwich van needs washing every second day – a dirty van gives the wrong image.

- You will spend a surprising amount of time on your feet, and not just serving your customers. Once your selling day is over, you will spend several days each week visiting supermarkets or wholesalers and completing the general tasks involved in running a business.

Basically, it's pretty much non stop from when you load the van in the morning (and even earlier, if you make the sandwiches yourself) until you empty it and clean it in the afternoon. You may finish all your tasks, including supply purchasing and admin by 6pm, but you will feel you have worked a long physical day.

To do this on a daily basis takes stamina and high energy levels. Your fitness level is one aspect to consider, but other factors are equally important.

Stress levels

Running a sandwich round can involve as much stress as any other venture; aspects of the business will affect people differently. Probably the most common cause of stress is the crowd scenario.

And then you experience the lunchtime rush. Instead of the orderly trickle of people you are used to, a rapidly growing crowd gathers at the van, as if drawn by a magnet, all with limited time to wait, and all hungry...

More people to serve, more orders to add up, more ditherers to hurry along.....You watch in horror as the crowd grows even bigger, your heart beats faster and mild panic sets in...work faster! ...hand out the sandwiches, add the totals, take the money.....onto the next customer. Hurry Up! Time loses all meaning as you focus on the order at hand.

....and then it's all over, the crowd has gone, a few stragglers here and there, easy to handle them. You have survived!

Just about everybody in the sandwich trade has experienced this, to a varying degree. I used to dread big crowds and found it nerve wracking, but I eventually got more used to it. It helps if you visualize the approaching customer as a £5 note on legs.

As long as you are prepared for a degree of crowd stress, and can get reasonably used to it, you will be fine. Its worth knowing that even though a large crowd can gather very quickly, its rare for people to be unpleasant, they can see that you are working as quickly as possible.

Do you genuinely enjoy meeting people?

The vast majority of your customers will be polite, friendly and pleasant people. It's only fair that you present a smiling warm personality in return, even if the grins do become a little fixed towards the end of a long day.

Putting people at ease goes a long way to keeping them as long term customers, being moody is a guaranteed way to lose them.

Occasionally you will come across the dour unpleasant individual, and you will have to deal with it. You can't afford to be unpleasant or aggressive in return, it presents a bad image to the other customers and it will also ruin your day. A sandwich round is a public facing business, if you don't enjoy meeting or dealing with people one on one, you will struggle to keep your customers.

Do you like working with food?

If you don't have a genuine interest in the products you are selling, you are going to have a miserable business life, how will you maintain enthusiasm when you don't really have any interest? You might get by at first, but you will eventually grow to resent the business.

The public are more concerned about food quality than ever, how will you respond when questioned about:

- The source of your eggs – free range, battery, or free range organic?
- Do your cakes contain hydrogenated oils?
- What colourings or additives are in your foods?
- What are the sugar levels in your breads?

You have to have an interest in the food you sell, because a growing number of your customers will. There is a trend towards healthier eating and sandwiches are seen as a healthy alternative to traditional fast food, it follows that people will ask more questions as a result.

Do you have a positive outlook?

It's inevitable that you will encounter setbacks from time to time, can you bounce back? Or do you give up at the first sign of trouble? You must have a positive outlook on life, to counteract the little knocks.

Other considerations

Running a sandwich round doesn't need to be rocket science. You need determination, common sense and the ability to handle the basic management of your business. In this respect, it's just like any other commercial venture. There are numerous sources of information about the generalities of starting a business – from books to the small business department of your local bank.

Hygiene requirements

This is a vital subject which receives a lot of attention later in the book. There is one requirement you need to fulfil before you can legally work with food and that is to undertake a one day hygiene training course. Don't worry, it's very basic. Again, I detail this in the relevant chapter.

Adding up

You will need to be pretty nimble at adding up the orders, and handing back the correct change. It may take some practise until you are comfortable with this. When I started out, I took a calculator with me, you might like to do the same.

The Viability of the Business

This section outlines the research that needs to be done if you plan to start a sandwich round from scratch. If you intend buying an existing business, your investigations will be a little different and I cover that scenario in the next chapter.

Is there a demand for sandwich van rounds?

Well, the abundance of sandwich vans countrywide shows that on a basic level, the concept of starting and running a sandwich round is viable.

It's just a question of whether there is sufficient demand in your area for a new sandwich round – and that's where the research comes in. Firstly though, it would be useful to get some background information on the sandwich trade.

Getting to Know the Sandwich Market

You need to get a feel for what the sandwich trade is. The best way to accomplish this is by observing and learning from those already in the field.

What this comes down to, is stalking a few sandwich vans in different areas and taking note of how they operate. At first, keep your distance and watch how the van operator plies his trade. Take notes, rather than relying on memory. Don't make it blatantly obvious that you are there as an observer.

I used to take photos whenever possible. It's quite legal to take photographs in a public area, but you don't really want to be seen doing it.

Get a general feel for the atmosphere surrounding the van and the customers. Are the orders handled quickly? What techniques does the van driver have for dealing with the crowds? Does the whole process seem efficient, or can you see obvious areas for improvement? After a few sessions observing from afar, you will need to make contact with the van operator, acting like any other paying customer. This gives you the chance to examine the actual food that is being sold, the packaging, and the layout of the interior.

Some other points to consider should be:

- The menus that various vans offer and the prices.
- How do the prices vary between different vans?
- Is the quality of the food acceptable, how generous are the filling portions? What is the freshness like?
- The types of vans, and the appearance of them. Do they look drab and worn?

- What about the packaging, is it embossed with the company logo? Do they even have a logo?

- What approach do the van operators take to sign writing? Does it stand out?

- Do any of the vans offer something special, not available at their competitors?

- What does the average order consist of?

- What is the customer profile, office workers? Site workers? And do they order the same things?

Sandwich autopsy

Try and get hold of as many menus as you can, from the vans you visit. Not only will this give you inspiration for your own menu, but it will help you get a feel for the pricing structure in your area.

When I first started out, I lost count of the number of sandwiches I bought and took home for complete dissection, carefully noting the construction and portion layout of each. I even took photographs for future reference! It was the best way of learning about sandwich creation, labelling and packaging, and I thoroughly recommend you do exactly the same.

Incidentally, keep the sandwich packaging. It's handy to compare how various sellers approach this issue.

Get a free education

There is another way to learn a great deal about the sandwich trade in a short space of time. Pretend you are looking for a business to buy, and then visit those that are for sale. You may not be able to find a complete sandwich round for sale at the time of your research, in which case locate a few vans instead. A good place to start is E-Bay. Once you have found a few that are reasonably local, pay the owners a visit.

The owners will usually tell you everything you want to know, it's like a free education. It's a good way to find out the profit percentages on sandwiches, cakes, cookies and cool drinks in your neck of the woods, this is relevant and handy information to have.

As well as interrogating the owner about the trade, you get to examine a sandwich van close up, in full detail – not with the intention of buying one at this stage- but rather to learn about the various types of refrigeration, warming cabinets, and general layout etc.

You might feel a bit guilty about wasting the owner's time, but its all part of the business game, and it could happen to you one day!

Sandwich and Snack News Magazine

A very useful periodical for those in the trade, available only on subscription and published every second month. Give them a call and ask for a free evaluation copy, they can be reached on (01291) 636338. Information on trends, hygiene, and the sandwich industry in general are their stock in trade. You could pick up some useful tips and ideas, so it's worth considering a subscription. The website is www.sandwich.org

Internet searches

Another source of information that you should use is the internet, the data available is staggering, visit the websites of sandwich based businesses and take note of any ideas that you could use, copy or modify.

Researching profit margins

Typically, a sandwich purchased from a van will have a margin of 55-75 %. Cakes and cookies offer about the same. Most of the other menu items such as cold drinks or crisps offer lower percentages. Coffee, tea and soup (if you are equipped to sell it) can easily offer margins of 100% or more. The overall average, for all products, probably runs at about 65% or thereabouts in my experience.

The prices you set for some of your products will in part be determined by what your rivals charge. For example, it wouldn't be wise to charge 30p more for a can of coke than anyone else does – you need to stay in the ball park with common stock items like that, customers will resent paying over the odds.

Sandwiches tend to be bought on the basis of quality, rather than price (unless the price is truly excessive). Don't make the mistake of assuming you need to have the lowest prices around, rather concentrate on using better quality ingredients.

This was brought home to me quite clearly in my early days by a disgruntled customer, who commented:

'Everyone seems to use the cheapest sausages they can find, I'd pay double for a decent sausage sandwich'

Did I take note of what he said? You bet I did, it was my first lesson that people put quality over price when it comes to sandwiches. From then on, any sausage sandwich sold from my van was created using Cumberland's finest – it cost more, but it certainly wasn't double.

Daily turnover

This can only be a guideline. Lots of different factors come into play. But I can give you an idea, based on my experience, together with information I have gleaned from business owners over the years. Assuming you were the only sandwich van visiting two or three large office parks or industrial estates, you could expect between £500 and £800 a day. However, very few operators are lucky enough to have the whole pie to themselves. Most van owners do not turnover more than £350 a day.

Decide if this is the business for you

Before too long, your knowledge of the sandwich trade is going to be pretty extensive. You'll have a fair idea if a similar business is really for you. Even at these early stages you should be considering your unique angle, what you can do to stand out from your competitors.

This is a very important aspect of the business and the chapter titled 'Establishing your Identity' covers it in detail.

Research – before you Start the Business

Once you have gained some background information on the sandwich trade and decided that you like the idea of being part of it, it's time to start some serious investigation. As a sandwich round operator, your main markets will be office parks and industrial estates, because these tend to be located away from supermarkets and other retailers likely to be selling sandwiches.

You would find it hard to sell sandwiches to workers in an office block if a Marks and Spencer's was located next door, because the workers would probably just pop out at lunch time to grab something to eat. The big selling point of a sandwich round is convenience. Workers get hungry and you bring food to them – that's a useful service when there's no place close by to feed them.

Market research

This is, without a doubt, the most important section of the entire book. How you decide to proceed, once you have read the information I present, could determine whether your business succeeds or fails.

I know that sounds dramatic, but it's true. If you spend money buying a van, getting supplies and possibly even fitting out a commercial kitchen, you need to know that you can sell your products. What happens if nobody buys from you? Or the business park that looked like a goldmine has a blanket ban on sandwich vans of any type? Or too many vans already prowl the territory?

Unfortunately, I speak from bitter experience. I did very little market research – and was very nearly out of business within the first week. My first day running a sandwich van went something like this:

I set off with a nicely stocked brand new van, plenty of sandwiches on board (where the sandwiches and stock came from is a story for a later chapter) and drove in the general direction of a large local industrial estate. I wasn't sure about the best time to approach customers, but reckoned just before 10am might be a good starting point.

Parking outside a suitable looking building, I hopped out of the van and entered the reception area. The receptionist looked up guardedly as I approached.

'Hello, I run a sandwich van and I will be calling at the estate every day at about this time, would it be OK if I

parked outside and tooted the horn to let people know I'm here?'

'I can call at reception, instead of hooting if that's more convenient?' I added helpfully.

The look she gave me suggested exasperation, tinged perhaps with a hint of pity.

'You can if you think it's worth it, but three sandwich vans already call here every day'.

For a second or two I stood there in stunned horror. Then I thanked her and went back to the van, shaken and very, very worried. I called at other businesses on the estate and visited two other office parks that day. It was the same story every time – they didn't need another sandwich van.

It was becoming clear that I hadn't done enough research. I had spent more time dreaming up menus and planning a website, than actually investigating if a market even existed.

Buying that van had wiped out my life savings. I was facing some serious problems.

Knock on doors

It doesn't take a brain surgeon to see what I should have done. Before spending a single pound, I should have visited as many business parks and offices as possible and *asked* if any vans were currently visiting.

I can state truthfully, that If I had done this and seen how over saturated my local market was, I wouldn't have spent £25,000 pounds buying a brand new sandwich van.

It can be daunting, because it's basically a form of cold calling and nobody likes doing it, but you absolutely have to get out there and knock on doors if you want to avoid the mistakes I made.

If the local market is saturated, then what?

It's highly unlikely that you will find a business park or industrial estate that has no sandwich or other food vans calling. You have to accept there will be competition.

If the location gets visited by one or two vans, then you should be able to carve out a niche for yourself – specialising in hot food, or French Baguettes, or some other unique angle that gives you a selling edge over the competition. However, if three or more vans already service a territory, it's probably better to look elsewhere. It will be a struggle to establish a viable business when your rivals are so well entrenched.

I had to relocate to another town in order to find business parks that offered reasonable sales. I didn't have a lot of choice. It was either that, or sell the van at a big loss. If you find out that your local market seems saturated *before* buying an expensive van, you won't have to take such drastic action

An alternative approach

If your 'knocking on doors' research shows that your choice of territories is oversupplied with sandwich vans and you don't want to travel further afield , there is an untapped market that most largish towns have. It's the small business parks with perhaps 10-12 companies on them.

The more established vans don't usually bother with them, since the takings are considered to be too small. But these businesses are usually very glad to have someone visiting them, and can make loyal customers.

Inevitably, there will be more driving between stops, using more fuel which has to be taken into account. This can be offset by raising your prices slightly to compensate. It's very likely you will find numerous smaller territories with little or no competition – your slightly higher prices will not lead to lost sales.

During my first few months, I found plenty of these smaller territories and made lots of regular sales. Unfortunately taking £150 a day, when you have just spent £25,000 on a new van is never going to be viable.

However, if your van costs £2500 or £3000 then that turnover can leave you with an acceptable profit.

The competition

Chat to the people who work on the business parks or estates and you'll learn about the types of food vendors that visit.

If three food vans visit a business park, selling burgers, fish and chips, and sandwiches respectively, they are all competition. But only the sandwich van is competing directly with your product range – there would be enough room for the two of you on a large estate.

Any business that sells the same (or very similar) products as you can be classified as direct competition. In the sandwich world, that can be supermarkets, newsagents, petrol stations and even vending machines. Fortunately, business parks with supermarkets or petrol stations are the exception rather than the norm.

As you carry out your local research, you will come into contact with some of the larger franchise operators, don't be put off and think you can't compete with them. There are thousands of small sandwich rounds, earning comfortable livings for their owners.

Always remember that as an independent, you have the flexibility that the large franchises can only dream about. You can change your prices, menu, or anything else on the spur of the moment. Variety is the spice of life, and it's something that customers appreciate.

There will always be opportunities for small independents offering a varied and varying menu together with that sense of individuality that the big chains just cannot match.

Just speak to the customers

Whilst I agree that there are plenty of ways to gain information (from banks to the internet) you cannot beat the 'knocking on doors' method. It's the only way to get conclusive answers about your potential sales and the existing competition.

Whatever else you do, get out there and talk to your potential customers. It might take a couple of weeks to gather information, but you will gain invaluable data about the state of the market and the best way to establish a viable business.

Chapter Three

A Look at Your Business Options

A Few Points to Consider

It's one thing deciding that you want to go into the sandwich business, it's quite another deciding on the best way to do it. Essentially you have three options open to you.

- Purchase an existing business and take it on as a 'Going Concern'.
- Buy a Franchise.
- Start your own business from scratch.

This book focuses on starting your own business, rather than buying a franchise or taking over a going concern. It's how I entered the sandwich trade and I firmly believe it's the best option for most people.

However, I am also aware that starting a business from scratch is not for everyone, so a few words on the other options open to you would be in order.

Buying an Existing Sandwich Round

There is no denying that buying a business outright is the quickest way to enter the market. On the surface, it also looks to be the easiest option, certainly your workload might be less than when starting from scratch. The advantages of buying an established business can be considerable, but there are potentially major downsides as well.

A sandwich round business might consist of little more than one van and a list of sites that the operator visits on a daily basis. Or you might be purchasing many vans and taking on the lease of a commercial kitchen where your sandwiches are made. Whatever the scale of the venture, a lot of careful investigation will be needed.

Advantages

- Getting finance should be easier because the business is already an established and proven operation.

- There will be (or should be) an established customer base. The business should have a good reputation.

- The business should be profitable, and creating an income, without you needing to alter the basic operation.

- Existing employees will be experienced and you can draw on their knowledge.

Disadvantages

- The condition of vehicles and equipment might not be as you anticipated. You won't easily be able to judge the mechanical condition until you have actually taken possession of the business.

- There could be hidden problems, which the seller is unlikely to reveal and this may lead to additional complications or expenses down the line.

- There could be problems with existing staff, which you would be obliged to solve. You can't just renew the employee base when you take over. The existing employees have a multitude of rights to protect their interests.

- It's possible that the seller knows of outside developments that could affect the viability of the business, if you or your legal team don't pick up on them, the long term future of the business could be doubtful.

- It could be that the profitability of the business has been falling for a long while. The trend might continue, regardless of what you do. Perhaps the competition is so intense that the seller has decided to sell up. You might struggle to turn the business around.

Minimise the Danger

Buying a business might seem the easiest way to get started but it can be fraught with dangers. You can reduce the risks by seeking professional advice.

You will need guidance on how to value a business, including its intangible assets. The financial strengths and weaknesses must be analysed. You also need to find out why the business is being sold. Engaging the services of an accountant and a lawyer specialising in commercial law are two essential steps for anyone thinking about buying a business.

Some proprietors claim to deliberately underestimate their takings, in order to reduce their tax bill. Don't fall for this trick, even though it's prevalent. You can only judge the profitability of a business by analysing the accounts, and seeing how much tax has actually been paid over the years. Before choosing to start a sandwich round from scratch, I did consider buying a going concern. But one point eventually stopped me. It struck me that buying someone else's businesses also meant buying all their problems too.

Taking on a Franchise

Typically the owner of a business (the franchisor) grants a person the right to trade using their business model, brand name and ideas. In exchange for this, the franchisee pays an initial fee and an annual royalty to the franchisor. Quite often the person taking out the franchise will only be granted the right to trade in a specific geographical area.

Who would run a franchise?

If a person wants to run a business, but is not confident of their ability to get things off the ground, then a franchise could be the answer. Basically, the franchisor will guide you every step of the way. The end result is that your business will be virtually identical in look and operation to the rest of the chain.

Your van will be stocked with the franchisor's product range. As with any other business choice, there are pros and cons to consider, before you decide if franchising is the best way forward for you.

Advantages of taking on a franchise

- You get to open your business on a proven business model.

- Advice and information should be readily available.

- You won't have to be concerned with kitting out a van or finding supplies, this is all taken care of for you.

- You may be able to speak to other franchisees about their experiences – before committing to a franchise.

- Less time will be spent on the basics and more on the day to day running of the business.

- The benefit of an established brand should translate into higher sales through increased customer confidence.

Disadvantages

- You will have to pay an upfront sum, which is called the initial franchise fee. This sum is non-refundable if the business doesn't work out. In addition to this, there is usually an annual royalty due as well, normally a percentage of sales. The initial fee can be anything from £7000 to £20,000. For a business start up, this is serious capital.

- There is very little flexibility in the business model. You have to stick to the guidelines laid down by the franchisor, you can't change the van décor or the menu, for example. If you enjoy creativity, this can be stifling. More importantly, you are restricted to selling the official product range – which means your profit is restricted.

- If there is friction between the franchisor and the franchisee, the latter invariably comes off worse. Arguments or disagreements can cause big headaches for the franchisee. At times like this, you realise that running a franchise doesn't really make you the boss, you are still answerable to others. Surely the idea of independence was a factor in deciding to become self employed?

- Not all franchises have a happy ending. If the holding company folds, or has a policy change, you could be facing an uncertain future.

Search the internet for information about sandwich van franchising and you will discover a legal battle taking place between a major sandwich shop chain (which has decided to enter the sandwich van market by selling franchises) and some of the people who bought franchises from the company.

As part of the agreement, the van operators sell only products supplied by the company – with low profit margins available. This has resulted in more than a few of the franchisees selling sandwiches from other sources, in the hope of increasing their profit. Litigation is now in progress and the whole situation is turning very ugly.

Running a franchise is still hard work

Please don't assume that buying a franchise equates to an easy ride. Far from it, you will have to work just as hard as someone who starts from the ground up. A franchise is definitely not a passport to easy riches and short working hours – even though many franchisors would say otherwise.

If you are interested in franchising then contact the 'British Franchise Association' who can provide you with the ins and outs of the franchising world. Their number is 01865 379892 or log on at http://www.thebfa.org/. Stick to those with a proven track record, who willingly allow you to contact their existing franchisees.

A final point on franchising. Do you really *want* someone to hold your hand and lead you all the way? Isn't half the fun and satisfaction doing it yourself and creating your own business, rather than just following someone else's lead?

Starting Your Business From Scratch

I carried out a lot of research before deciding that I wanted to start from the ground up. It wasn't a decision that was taken lightly. Several businesses were visited and examined in detail – some with high price tags.

None of them really caught my imagination (but I did gain a lot of useful information) and I couldn't shake the feeling that I would be paying over the odds for the goodwill of these established sandwich rounds. This was a major factor against buying a going concern.

The advantages of starting your own sandwich round

- The money you spend will go towards the actual business start up costs, there won't be any 'Goodwill' to pay. When you buy a going concern, you are paying for the fact that the business already has a customer base. The goodwill of this customer base is often hard to conclusively value.

- Your menus will be set by you. There will be no established customer base to wean onto a new product range.

- The van and other equipment will be either new or from known sources, not someone else's 'clapped out junk', with potential mechanical faults.

- The satisfaction of actually starting a business is greater than just buying an existing one.

The disadvantages

- It can be harder to raise finance, lenders are usually more wary of business start ups.

- The process of starting a business involves a lot of steps, each requires co-ordination. You will function as overall project manager. This means handling all aspects, from finding a van and other equipment, to sorting out premises (if you decide to kit out a commercial kitchen) and dealing with tradesmen.

- Costs can rise unexpectedly unless you keep a firm grip on them.

- There is a danger that you spend forever investigating and researching, without ever actually committing to the business.

Starting your own business can be daunting, but if you break the whole project down into small steps, the concept does become manageable. A flow chart offers a practical way to lay out each step of the business process, it's a method chosen by a lot of new business people.

Put it onto paper

The important thing is to put all of your ideas and thoughts onto paper, and take it from there. It's the best way of organising everything into a kind of logical order. You can't keep it all in your head, performing a juggling action from one thought to another.

I simply used an A4 pad and wrote a list of what had to be done. As each task was completed, it was crossed off. It might sound simplistic, but it worked for me. This won't be the only list you make, but it can be the master one. The major tasks on your list should correspond fairly closely to the chapters in this book, although the order you carry them out might differ.

Hard Work but Satisfying

I can't pretend that starting a business is easy, it's hard work and there will be times when you are dog tired, stressed out and irritable, when nothing goes right and you doubt your own sanity for starting out in the first place.

Despite this, and admittedly I am somewhat biased, I believe the satisfaction and other benefits you get from creating your own business cannot be equalled by taking on a franchise or buying a going concern.

Sources of Advice and Information

Before starting a business, you should do as much research on the basics as possible. I don't mean the basics of the sandwich trade, that's what this book is for. I am referring to the business and management basics that apply to all new ventures.

Nowadays more than ever, there are plenty of sources to help you get off the ground. Over the past ten years or so, small business development has become a serious issue.

Major high street banks

Most of the major banks have a section that deals specifically with the needs of small businesses. They can provide you with start up information and advice on all aspects of the venture.

Chamber of commerce

You're local chamber of commerce – an invaluable source of information for the new and established business person.

Business Link

Many worthwhile publications are available for download on www.businesslink.gov.uk, I regard this as one of the finest websites for the budding small business person. Information is laid out clearly and concisely.

The Department of Trade and Industry

Although this site is directed at the business world in general, it is the key website for anything business related and should be on your list. The information available to browse is truly vast. You can log on at www.dti.gov.uk

Business management course

The more research you do, the easier your business life will be. For example when you deal with your accountant or solicitor, you will save a lot of time (and fees) if they don't have to explain the basics of business to you. Since this information is available online and for free, it makes sense to take advantage of it. However, it can make good sense to take a business course as well. A formal course is a superb way of getting a lot of information in a structured and measured way. If you can spare the time and if this is your first business venture, it's worth considering.

Your Business Format

At some point, you will have to decide what format your business will take. For example, will you operate as a sole trader, a limited company or maybe go into partnership? This decision will depend on your own circumstances. Do speak to an accountant before making any firm decisions, as your own situation could have a major influence on the best way of proceeding.

The popular choice

The majority of small business people choose to operate as a sole trader, there are clear advantages over the other options. Again, at the risk of repeating myself, contact an accountant who can examine your personal tax circumstances and advise on the best way to proceed.

Your Name and Image

If you want your business to stand out from the crowd, you have to offer more than just good food. In this day and age you need a professional image and identity. On a very basic level, this means having a respectable looking van and keeping it clean and presentable – but there is a bit more to it than that.

Choosing a Business Name is a Priority

You can't leave this until the last moment. You may be tempted to wait until the business is nearing completion, and hope that inspiration strikes, but that is the wrong way to approach the issue. Long before you begin trading, you will be dealing with at least some of the following:

- Suppliers
- The bank
- Health department
- Inland revenue
- Electricians / Plumbers / Builders
- Solicitors / accountants / surveyors / landlord

That list isn't exhaustive. All of these dealings will involve paperwork, from invoices to contracts. Life will be a lot easier if your business name is sorted out early on.

A few pointers on choosing a name

As long as you adhere to a few basic guidelines, you can choose any name you want. Simply use common sense and you won't go far wrong.

- Choose a name that is easy to say, preferably only a few words long.

- Generally avoid humour in the name, it may be funny for a while, but can soon get boring, and then you are stuck with it. I will admit that there is a fish shop in Wales with the name `A Fish Called Rhonda` which does tickle me, but examples like this are quite rare and even this could become tedious after a while.

- Don't choose a name that limits you. You may think 'A Taste of Italy' sounds impressive, but what if you change your menu to include substantially more American sandwich lines, or worse still, stop selling Italian style sandwiches altogether ?

Use your competitors for inspiration, but avoid slavishly copying them – there is no point in provoking legal action.

The Right Image is Crucial

A sandwich based business has to project an image of wholesomeness, quality and cleanliness. In the past, that's all you would have needed, but unfortunately nowadays image and brand are often seen as more important that the product being sold.

That doesn't mean you can offer poor food and make up for it with a glossy brand new van, that certainly won't work, but it does mean that your business will need a corporate image in addition to an excellent menu.

So how are you going to project the right image? Bear in mind that customers will have judged your business before they even get very close to the van, and first impressions count hugely. Since your van is your shop, it must look clean and professional. In addition to this, signwriting is a must.

Vehicle signwriting

In the past few years the cost of creating professional decals in vinyl has fallen to such an extent that you can now get your van signwritten for as little as £90. This can include high quality graphics, logos and even photos.

A quick browse of the internet will reveal plenty of companies to contact for a quote and / or help with the design. For the ultimate in style, you could opt for a custom airbrush paint job, but it's costly and not really necessary.

It's very important that your van stands out at a distance and is immediately identifiable by its signwritten name. If you don't have clear and visible markings it's going to be hard to build up a recognizable identity – and you need to be recognized the instant you park up outside a business.

You have to make it as easy as possible for customers to remember you. There is a second reason why large clear markings are vital. If a competitor invades your territory with a similar van, and also has no markings, he could steal some of your sales. You might think that sounds a bit far fetched, but it's a tactic I used a few times at the very beginning.

I didn't get my van signwritten at first and I noticed that a rival was using a similar van, also without signwriting. I decided to invade his patch and grab some of his sales. This was fairly easy, if a little nerve-wracking. I visited his customers 10 minutes earlier than he did and tooted the horn to announce my presence.

Customers spilled out of the buildings and reached my van before realising I wasn't the usual sandwich man. Some turned around and went back inside, no doubt to await the arrival of the 'Real McCoy', but others bought from me anyway. It's possible that some didn't realise I wasn't the regular.

This practise definitely cost the usual operator sales. If his van had been clearly signwritten, his customers would have spotted him from a distance – and my scheme wouldn't have worked.

It's possible that just by turning up I would have made some sales anyway. But it's a fact that customers don't easily switch their allegiances from a proven regular van to an untried newcomer.

I am not suggesting that you use this tactic to get sales; hopefully you followed my advice on market research and won't need to resort to such desperate measures. Rather, I am hoping to stop you falling victim to this by stressing the importance of getting your van signwritten before you sell a single sandwich.

That way, you are building your brand image from day one, and presenting a memorable identity to your expanding customer list – with the added benefit of preventing a clone stealing your sales.

Your Logo and Look

Getting a professional look and projecting the right image does not mean you must spend a fortune, or give up on the idea of being an independent and buy a franchise.

You do need a logo and a colour scheme, not just for your vehicle signwriting, but also for your sandwich packaging, menus and website. It all has to blend together with the intention of establishing your brand.

As an independent, you have to do all the work. You have to design your own logo and think up your own colour scheme, as well as choosing how many colours to use.

The good news is that you can actually buy ready made logos from companies that specialise in creating them. Just type "Logo creation "or "Buy Logo" into a search engine and you can preview and choose from hundreds. The price can be anything from £50 and that is good value for money, when the alternative might be to use a professional design agency.

Getting creative

Spend some time investigating the competition. What approaches do your rival sandwich round operators take to logo and colour designs?

Don't neglect sandwich shops. Both the independents and franchised operators could have useful ideas that you could borrow and adapt to suit your requirements. Have a look at other businesses, the best ones use simple eye catching designs, without going over the top.

Use the internet, look at other sandwich businesses in other parts of the world; you could pick up some very nice ideas to incorporate into your venture.

Keep the colour scheme simple and avoid heavy clashing or contrasts. A point to bear in mind is that when it comes to printed matter (such as menus) a two colour design is much cheaper than one with three or more colours.

Don't forget that at some point you might start wearing T-shirts or tops with your business logo and colours – so it makes sense to choose colours you would be happy to wear.

Using a design consultant

If you are stuck for creative inspiration then calling in the experts could be an option, there are companies that could take care of everything for you.

Your entire look, image, colour scheme and logo could be custom designed especially for you. Some of them are very good and could undoubtedly come up with an image that you are happy with. However, you are going to pay for their advice and expertise.

I would suggest that if you are creative enough to start your own sandwich company (you are, because you are reading this book) then you are certainly able to design your own logo and colour scheme, or choose a ready made one, without spending much needed cash on design consultant fees.

Establishing Your Identity

The purpose of the signwriting, logos and corporate colours, is to help customers recognize and remember you – to make you stand out from the competition. However, you need to give them a reason to remember you and you do that by establishing your unique identity.

Your identity is how you want your customers to see you. How will they 'identify' you as being different from your competitors?

Create a niche

If your sandwiches and other product lines are the same as your rivals, then there is no incentive for customers to sample your offerings. You have to try and separate yourself from the ordinary. You don't have to go to extremes; you just need that special 'something' that makes you stand out.

When a customer complained that he couldn't get a decent sausage sandwich anywhere, I listened and acted. Before long, I had established my identity as the van with the best sausage sandwiches you could buy. Your unique angle could be equally simple, listen to your customers and maybe pickup some useful ideas.

You probably have some ideas already, perhaps you will become known as the king of exotic cheese fillings, or maybe your stuffed turkey sandwiches just can't be beaten.

Only you can choose your identity. You might change your mind several times before finding your special niche, don't let this bother you, it's perfectly normal.

Chapter Four

The Sandwich Van in Detail

Your sandwich van is basically a mobile shop and like a shop it needs to display your products to the buying public. If you don't have a visible display area, then you are going to have a hard time attracting customers when parked.

Sandwich vans fall into two camps – those that are professionally manufactured for food vending and those that are basically fridge vans.

- Fridge vans – typically a panel van. Customers are served from the rear of the vehicle. There are no side displays.

- Professional sandwich van – has side hatches that open to reveal display of goods. Transit size vans often have rear display as well.

Fridge Vans

Any van with a refrigerated compartment can be called a fridge van. A lot of people do use them for retailing sandwiches, despite the fact that access is usually from the rear, without any form of display in place.

Quite often, sandwiches and other goods are stored in boxes that the customers rummage through looking for something to eat.

Suitability for a sandwich round?

If you are serious about making a decent income from your sandwich round, you need to give fridge vans a miss. Rather consider purchasing a professionally designed van which offers a way to display your goods. Fridge vans are designed as transport vehicles, not as mobile shops.

This kind of van would be ideal if you were delivering sandwiches wholesale. Because in that scenario the vehicle does not need to attract customers, it is merely a sandwich delivery van.

Professionally Manufactured Vans

A modern sandwich van can be used for selling much more than cold sandwiches. Hot food such as pies and pasties or bacon baps can all be retailed successfully. Some vans even have coffee machines and soup urns installed.

From a customer point of view, the display cabinets that showcase your products form the focal point of the vehicle. This is the main advantage of a van designed specifically for food retailing – the public can see and appreciate your product range, easily and quickly.

Sandwich van manufacturers know that it's important to create high quality food display cabinets. Stainless steel and glass is used in the construction of these displays in order to mimic the appearance of a retail store. Subtle lighting and even piped music add to the professional image.

Van Choices

Sandwich vans vary in size and carrying capacity. The smallest (if you exclude fridge panel vans) tend to be based on the little 1.3 litre Daihatsu. Further up the chain you will find mid-size vans between 1.6 - 2.0 litres, with carrying capacities of around 200kg. Sandwich trucks exist that can carry 500Kg of food and drinks – generally only needed by people with well established rounds. When you are establishing your round, a mid-size van is a good choice.

Sandwich vans are often referred to as 'Jiffy Trucks'. This is a generic term for any van with a stainless steel box bolted onto the back, with side opening canopies that are raised to reveal the food displays.

Despite the generic name, Jiffy is a manufacturer of vans with a history going back thirty years. A genuine Jiffy Truck is a high quality vehicle – don't just assume that any white van with a stainless steel box on the back is a genuine Jiffy, there are lots of clones out there.

Features of a Typical Sandwich Van

Any modern sandwich van will have a selection of the features listed in the next sections. My definition of modern is any vehicle produced in the last 10 years or so.

Refrigerated display

The refrigerated compartment generally consists of a display area, used for the actual products on sale, and spare space for storing bulk items that you might need later in the day. For example if you need to refill the cold drinks display.

I will explain some of the technical workings later in the chapter, but for now, suffice to say that it's as easy to operate as a car air-conditioner (actually its even easier).

Heated Food warmer

The majority of professional sandwich vans are fitted with food warmers. It's important to note that a warmer is not an oven; you cannot use it to cook food, only to heat up pre-cooked products such as pies or sausage rolls. Older systems were gas powered, with a portable gas tank being the source. Newer systems use a diesel heat exchanger setup, powered by the battery and taking diesel from the fuel tank. In general this is a far superior system.

Bain Maries

These are stainless steel containers that hold hot food and keep it warm. You would use them for storing sausages, bacon, baked beans, rice or anything not suited to just sitting in the heated cabinet. They would be located within the heated display, usually on a runner system.

Ambient Storage

You have to have storage that is neither heated nor chilled for stock such as crisps, chocolates or sweets. Usually shelving is provided above the refrigerated section.

Side opening panel

The side opening panel gets raised to reveal the serving counter and the food displays. Most mid-size vans have one opening panel, and it would be fitted to the passenger side of the vehicle. Usually it's on hydraulic lifters, with a safety catch to prevent it closing down on anyone. A warning buzzer would normally be installed in the cab to prevent the vehicle being driving off with the panel still raised.

In winter time, or when it's raining, you and your customers will appreciate the side opening panel which acts as a shelter against the rain. Larger vehicles are often fitted with side opening panels on both sides of the van.

Hot Water and Sink

If your vehicle has the capacity to serve unpackaged hot food, for example a baked potato, then by law you must have a source of hot water and a sink to wash your hands in. Usually a small electrically operated heater is fitted with the waste water collected in a container beneath the sink. You could allow the waste water to drain away, but many local authorities take a dim view of this.

Electronic control panel

This is the digital control device that allows you to switch on the fridge unit, food warmer and heater for the sink. Usually it will also display the temperature of the fridge, not the heated warmer, as that will generally have a separate dial display within the hot food cabinet.

As a rule, the temperature settings for the fridge and heated cabinets are preset, all you have to do is switch them on in the morning, when you start the vehicle and switch them off at the end of the day.

Interior safe

This is a very handy piece of equipment for storing excess notes that build up during the day. Not something I had installed on my van unfortunately, which meant stuffing tens and twenties in the glove box or my pocket during hectic periods - not the best solution.

Satellite tracker

If you are buying new, then this is likely to be a requirement of your insurance policy. Even if it isn't, then fit one anyway. If your vehicle is stolen and is found abandoned, you will get the vehicle back quickly. Otherwise you will face a long wait for an insurance claim to be settled, and your customers won't be getting fed.

Key Out System

This is a useful feature that allows the engine to stay running even when the key is not in the ignition. When you are parked up serving customers your vehicle engine must stay running in order to power the cooler and hot food displays.

Being able to remove the key and lock the front doors provides a security measure. It's just additional peace of mind and is one less thing to worry about. Otherwise, you always have to keep an eye out for any customer potentially raking through the front cab.

Other features

In addition to the features already listed, it's not unusual to find the following fitted as well – admittedly generally to the larger vans, but not always.

- Dual sinks – one for hand washing and the other for utensils.
- Coffee machine – capable of producing quality beverages.
- Microwave oven.
- Soup urn.
- Hot water urn.

Buying a Van

Your first decision will be whether to buy new or used. There are pros and cons to consider, but don't assume from the word go that you need to buy a new van – buying used can be a sensible option.

One word of caution. Don't believe that buying a bigger van, with a huge carrying capacity will equate to bigger profits. It doesn't work that way. As a new start up, you should purchase a mid size vehicle. The typical engine size will be between 1.6 and 2.0 litre and the carrying capacity around 200kg. You don't need a vehicle the size of a Ford Transit. The larger sandwich trucks are designed for established operators who can sell enough to justify the increased carrying capacity – and running costs.

When buying used, you might be tempted by some of the smaller sandwich vans, typically built on the little 1.3 litre Daihatsu. There is nothing wrong with this, but in my experience the good ones cost almost as much as a decent mid size sandwich van.

Buying New

It's reasonable to expect a new sandwich van to have a lifespan of ten years or so. This does depend on the mileage being done each year, and how well it's looked after. Plenty of vehicles in circulation are older than this, and as long as you adhere to proper servicing and maintenance routines, you may be able to keep your van longer.

You will have the benefit of knowing that all of the equipment is brand new and under guarantee for at least one year. Often the vehicle itself will have a two or three year warranty, depending on mileage. Everything will look shiny and new, you won't have to put up with someone else's potentially worn out equipment.

Peace of mind is a precious thing. When you start your van in the morning you won't have to worry about older equipment that might fail during the day, leaving you with a non functioning fridge or hot display, or even worse, being stranded by the side of the road.

Having a new vehicle means a whole set of potential problems are put to one side, leaving you to concentrate on the running and expansion of the business. A new vehicle obviously costs more than a seven year old one, but those costs must be balanced against potential costs of the used vehicle.

Buying new doesn't necessarily mean paying cash up front, or even taking out a bank loan, there are other options available to help pay for the vehicle.

Ways of Paying for the Vehicle

There are several ways to pay for, or finance a new vehicle. Factors that will influence your decision will include the following:

- How much money can you raise as a deposit?
- Will you be VAT registered?
- Have you had a bad credit rating?
- Do you own your own home?
- Do you have large cash reserves?
- Will you drive the vehicle, or employ a driver?
- Have another source of income, or a business?
- What mileage will you be doing?
- How long do you intend to keep the vehicle?
- Do you intend to expand and purchase more vehicles?

These issues will need careful consideration before you can reach an informed decision about the best way to finance your purchase.

A Bank loan

With the current economic climate, it's very hard for small businesses to get bank finance unless they have significant assets behind them. Unfortunately banks only ever lend on their terms. They will always look for a way of recovering their money if they can foresee problems on the horizon.

If you are certain that you have enough working capital and will not need to approach the bank for a further loan, then you could consider this route.

Problems can arise if you run short of cash and approach them again; banks get nervous and generally tend to lend money when things are going well – if you start to struggle financially, getting further funds could be difficult.

If you plan to keep the vehicle for the long term and are going to be the main driver, then consider a bank loan, otherwise other options are better.

A Personal loan

This is generally a better option than a bank loan. You can borrow the whole amount that you need without having to find a deposit.

A charge will be placed against your home, but if this doesn't bother you, then this kind of financing is usually one of the cheaper choices. Like a bank loan, a personal loan is suited to the individual who will be an owner driver and intent on keeping the vehicle for the longer term.

Lease purchasing

This is the most common form of vehicle financing and is worth considering if you have a large deposit, or own your own home. There are serious tax advantages, but these are gained because legally you do not own the vehicle.

Usually ownership is transferred to you at the end of the agreement, for a nominal fee. You need to have a clean credit record to obtain favourable rates for the lease; otherwise you may find the agreement is more expensive than a bank loan.

Leasing is usually chosen by individuals or businesses that dispose of the vehicle after the lease agreement ends.

Contract hire

Fleet owners almost always choose this form of financing. The contract covers all maintenance, repairs and servicing. Even tyres are covered under this form of hire contract.

It would not cover breakdowns to specialised equipment such as refrigeration or heated displays. The other expenses that the hirer would bear are insurance and fuel.

With this form of contract hire, you do not own the vehicle, it belongs to the lender. Once the contract expires, it is given back. A new hire agreement would then be signed and a new vehicle issued.

If you are not going to be the main driver, or you are especially worried about mechanical problems, then this could prove a suitable option. The deposit should be nominal and the monthly payments reasonably low.

Paying cash

If you are going to drive the van yourself and keep it for the long term than this option is by far the cheapest. The resale of a properly maintained sandwich van can be surprisingly good, even if it is a few years old.

However, if you decide to sell the van after a few months because the business is not working, then you will take a big hit on the resale value. This is because the greatest depreciation in the vehicle value happens within the first few months.

Rent a vehicle

Before buying a new van, you may be offered the chance to rent one for a specified period. You pay a weekly charge and if the business doesn't work out, you hand the vehicle back, having only paid for the weeks you had it.

This offers a good way to, 'test the waters', of your new business. If everything goes as expected, then you buy a new van, otherwise you just hand the rental unit back and that is the end of the matter.

Buying a Used Sandwich Van

Naturally there are advantages to buying a used vehicle, but there are disadvantages too. Obviously the first consideration is price; a used vehicle will save you many thousands of pounds initially. The first owner has already suffered most of the depreciation just by driving the vehicle away from the forecourt.

When you in turn come to sell it, you are likely to suffer depreciation as well, but to a far lesser degree in pound terms. The biggest worry about buying used is that you may end up with a clapped out piece of junk.

If you need to sell the vehicle

If you have done your market research then you should already know if buying a sandwich van is a good idea or not.

But what if you have miscalculated and you realise within three weeks of operation that the competition is far more intense than you originally thought?

You may decide to sell the van and concentrate on other business pursuits. You could probably sell it without taking too much of a loss. To sell a brand new vehicle so soon would mean taking a huge financial knock, no question.

What to Look out for When Buying a Used Van

Essentially, buying a used sandwich van is much the same as buying any other form of small commercial vehicle. If you are not mechanically minded, then always take along someone who is when you visit the seller.

If you find a van that looks promising then you should seriously consider getting it professionally inspected. Naturally, you pay for this, but it could save you from making a costly mistake. Even if the inspection only throws up a few small, easily fixed problems, it does give you leverage when negotiating the price. If a seller does not welcome a professional inspection, then be suspicious.

Testing the Onboard Systems

A vehicle inspection service, as provided by organisations such as the AA or RAC, can be very useful in determining the mechanical condition of the van. They can check the engine, gearbox, suspension etc.

The onboard refrigeration and heated display systems may not fall within their area of expertise, so you'll have to satisfy yourself that all is in order.

The Refrigeration System

The majority of sandwich vans utilize a setup very similar to that of a standard car air-conditioning system. A crankshaft driven compressor, situated in the engine bay, pressurizes the refrigerant and distributes it to the rest of the refrigeration components.

I have heard of electric systems, not using an engine driven compressor, but have never seen one, and I believe they are quite rare.

Make sure the system cools

To test the system, make sure the engine is running, with the gear in neutral. Press the 'on' button to activate the chiller and check the digital temperature display - the control panel should be inside the cab, on the dashboard somewhere.

You will hear quite a loud noise as the refrigeration system kicks in. The readout should start dropping quickly until it reaches 3 or 4 degrees Celsius, which should be the pre-set chill range.

The pre-set may be a little lower than this, but should not drop below 1.5 degrees - you want chilled sandwiches, not deep frozen. Once the pre-set temperature is reached the system should switch off, it must not stay running.

You will hear some clicks from the engine bay as the compressor clutch disengages and then you should hear just the engine.

Let the system cycle a few times

After a few minutes, the temperature inside the chiller section will start to rise. When it reaches between 5 and 7 degrees the refrigeration system will kick in again and chill down to the preset of about 3 degrees or so. You need to watch and observe this cycle for a good fifteen to twenty minutes.

If you are testing the system in the middle of winter, then it is possible that the ambient temperature inside the chiller cabinet is too low for the refrigeration system to activate, if this is the case then wait for a warmer day.

Some older systems may have an adjustable pre-set temperature range. If the pre-sets are not acceptable, make sure you can adjust them from the control panel.

If you want to be absolutely sure that the temperature readouts in the chiller section are accurate, you can purchase a portable digital thermometer very cheaply. Place it in the chiller cabinet of the vehicle you are testing, and compare readings.

If the chiller fails to cool down, then it's probably best to avoid the vehicle. There are lots of components in a typical refrigeration setup, and pinpointing problems should be left to a specialist. Sorting out a problem could be as simple as re-gassing the system or it could mean a new compressor.

Beware of sellers claiming a re-gas is needed

If a vehicle has been standing for a long time and the refrigeration system has not been used, then it's possible that the compressor seals have dried out and allowed the refrigerant gas to escape.

This is a common scenario with cars, because the air-conditioning could stay unused for 6 months or so at a time. When this happens, all that is needed is a simple re-gas.

However, plenty of other components can cause problems. Don't necessarily believe a seller who says a faulty system needs a re-gas. It may actually need a compressor, which is generally an expensive fix.

The Hot Food Cabinet

If the vehicle has a hot food display it will most likely be powered by one of the following methods.

- Gas powered system – A portable gas cylinder is fitted to the vehicle and access to this is provided from outside the van.

- Engine heat powered – Excess heat from the vehicle engine is pumped to the hot food cabinet.

- Diesel powered - An electrically operated pump draws diesel from the main fuel tank into a heat exchanger, where it is mixed with air and burned. The air is then blown into the hot food display area.

Modern vans would either use the diesel heat exchanger, or the direct engine heat method. Portable gas systems tend to be found on older sandwich vans. The diesel system sounds complicated, but it's highly efficient and very popular.

Diesel Heat Exchanger Safeguard

If the vans diesel tank drops below a pre-determined level (usually about a quarter) then the heat exchanger system cuts out. This is a safeguard against a parked van running low on fuel and being stranded. If the system does cut out, it may need to be bled before it will function again. It's a lot less hassle to make sure your fuel tank is always a third or more full.

Testing the Heated Food Display

Testing the heated food display is simple, switch it on and wait for the temperature to rise. Within 15 minutes or so the temperature should be at about 80 degrees Celsius.

Legally, hot food has to be served at a minimum of 63 degrees Celsius in England and Wales - that refers to the food temperature, not the air temperature of your heated display. If your display heats much below 70-80 degrees, you are going to have a hard time serving hot food that meets the legal requirement, and your customers will complain about lukewarm pies.

Make sure that the Bain Maries heat up sufficiently and that the whole cabinet is evenly heated. As with the refrigeration test, it might be an idea to check the temperature independently with a digital thermometer.

Also, if the hot food cabinet is powered by gas and it has been disconnected, you will need to get it safety inspected.

Other Vehicle Systems

If your vehicle has a heated display and Bain Maries, it should also have a source of hot water and a sink fitted. Confirm that the onboard water heater gets hot and that the waste water container does not leak.

Check the sliding doors of the food displays, they should move smoothly and click closed securely. Make sure that the internal illumination of the food displays works properly – a blown bulb is a simple fix, tracing a wiring fault isn't.

The side panel that gets raised to show the food displays and serving counters is usually supported by hydraulic struts. These struts should be strong enough to support the entire weight of the panel without relying on the locking mechanism that gets applied when it's fully raised.

Used Vehicle Sources

You have several choices when it comes to buying a used sandwich van. You could buy from the original manufacturer, for example direct from Jiffy in Bradford. You could buy from a dealer specialising in catering vehicles, or you could buy privately.

Buying direct from the manufacturer

You are buying peace of mind here. The vehicle will have been thoroughly checked over and if necessary refurbished. It is likely to come with a generous warranty as well as back up if needed.

The price you see advertised is likely to be the price you pay, the lead times for sandwich trucks are long, and the manufacturers do not often need to offer discounts to induce sales of their second hand stock.

You will still save money over the advertised list price of a new unit though. Generally the vehicles available will be low mileage models, often sold back to the manufacturer by customers who have decided that a new sandwich van was not ideal for them.

The manufacturer will also be able to organise delivery on a door to door basis – which can be a major timesaver.

Catering truck specialists

The average dealer may have half a dozen available at any one time - varying in age from nearly new, to models over ten years old. It would be reasonable to expect a warranty on any purchase, as well as back up if needed.

The stock they carry could come from any source. Nearly new vans would probably be from people who have decided to sell because either the purchase was a mistake in the first place, or circumstances force them to sell. Quite often the vehicle would still be under the manufacturer's warranty.

Older vehicles are often traded in by established businesses as they upgrade to newer models - usually after they have been heavily worked. If you are lucky you may find a low mileage van being sold due to retirement, but you certainly cannot count on it.

Auctions

There are auction companies that specialise in selling catering equipment. From time to time, sandwich vans will appear in the lot listings. I would advise extreme caution if you are considering this course of action.

There is a thriving market in all types of mobile catering vans, quite often the ones that end up at auction are the ones that are unsaleable for one reason or another, don't be the one left holding a lemon.

I have seen sandwich vans for sale at big auction houses; presumably they are entered by companies selling off lease vehicles. I would still advise caution, if these vehicles were that good then they would have been sold off to the trade.

There are too many systems that need to be tested on a sandwich van for you to take a chance on buying completely 'as is'. Let someone take the risk.

Take an expert with you

If you decide to try your luck at auction, then its best to take along someone who knows a bit about vehicles, even if they are not a sandwich van expert.

I attended an auction a few years back where one of the lots was for a rather nice looking Jiffy Truck, not more than four years old. Bidding was fairly intense and the final price seemed to offer the bidder a good deal, assuming that the untested equipment all worked.

My brother, a bit of an expert on mechanical matters, was with me at the time and he pointed out that:

A: The vehicle was not a genuine Jiffy Truck – it was a clone.

B: The vehicle did not have an evaporator unit fitted for cooling down the fridge display, in fact it did not have a refrigeration system fitted at all!

The bid price for the van indicated that the potential owner was unaware of this fact. The only way he was going to chill his sandwiches was with pre-chilled cooler bags placed at the bottom of the fridge display!

My advice is to tread with extreme caution when it comes to auctions. It's very easy to get caught out, and you have no comeback against the auction house.

Online auctions

An online auction such as EBay is not like a conventional car auction. You bid and if you are lucky you win. However, you also get to test-drive the vehicle before you hand over your money. In fact you can usually arrange to meet with the seller and thoroughly check over the van before the auction even ends.

This is common practise and any genuine sellers will have no problem with it. The obvious rule is that if a seller won't allow you to test and check the vehicle before purchase, then you don't deal with him/her.

Buying privately

Buying privately is much the same as buying through an online auction such as EBay, the only difference is the medium used to advertise the vehicle. The same rules apply. Visit the seller and check the vehicle thoroughly before handing cash over.

Making a sandwich van

I cannot believe that I actually contemplated this. I seriously considered the idea of buying a van and turning it into a mobile food vehicle. I investigated everything from inverter powered hot cabinets, to glass sliding rail kits.

I will admit that everything you are likely to need to assemble your own creation does exist, without resorting to custom engineering in a big way, but it's not a practical option. The amount of time spent planning and constructing your own vehicle would seriously delay the actual business launch.

There are very few people who would be suited to taking on a project like this. I certainly wouldn't recommend it. Even if you had the expertise to do it, the cost savings would be negligible, and the final result would look less than professional. Leave van sandwich construction to the experts – they are the ones who do it for a living.

The Cheapest Option

Buying a van privately, either through an online auction or through a journal such as the 'Exchange and Mart', is the way to go if you are looking for the absolute cheapest price.

Some of the vans will be less than two years old. Others will be so new that they are virtually ex-demo. Vehicles this new are usually sold by people regretting their entry into the sandwich business and they are looking for a quick sale.

Older vehicles are also sold privately, often by people or companies upgrading to newer models. Typically these vans will have endured a hard life. You might be able to locate an older van being sold for 'genuine' reasons, but they are quite rare. More usually, an older vehicle is sold because it's no longer economic to maintain it.

Don't disregard the idea of buying a used vehicle from the manufacturer or a catering truck specialist. It's true that the price would be higher, but you get peace of mind.

Buying a brand new vehicle might be a good idea. However, my own experience leads me to believe that most people would be better off to avoid this option until they know that the business is going to succeed.

A new van is a huge investment. You have to decide whether you want to spend that kind of money upfront before you even have an established business, or wait until the business has proven itself.

Sandwich Van Insurance

Your insurance cover will be provided under a special category for catering vehicles. You cannot use ordinary motor insurance. In addition to this, you will need public liability insurance – in case the public are injured by your vehicle or the products you sell. I have always used a broker simply because it's easier and generally cheaper.

There is nothing stopping you organising your own insurance, just browse the web and you will be inundated with offers. Equally, there are plenty of brokers to choose from too.

Sandwich vans can be driven on an ordinary car licence and once you get used to the limited rear-view vision they are as easy to drive as any other small to medium size vehicle.

Sandwich Van Maintenance

If you buy a new vehicle, the manufacturer will outline the service intervals and the steps you need to take in order to maintain the van and your warranty. This would also apply if you purchase a used model from them. As long as you stick to the schedule problems should be few and far between.

However, if you plan to buy a van privately then it can get a little trickier. If the service handbook for the vehicle and onboard equipment is missing, you could try contacting the company that carried out the conversion in the first place. They might not have any printed matter available, depending on the age of the van, but they should be able to offer advice on the maintenance schedule.

What if the manufacturer cannot be located?

There are two aspects to maintaining a sandwich van.

- Vehicle servicing – as laid down by the manufacturer, such as Citroen or Mazda – which covers routine maintenance such as engine oil changes.
- The onboard systems servicing – as laid down by the company that converted the vehicle into a sandwich van. This would cover how and when to service the refrigeration display and hot food cabinet.

Phone your local Mazda or Citroen dealership (if that is the make of your van) and speak to someone in the servicing department. They will tell you how often to change the engine oil etc.

For information about the onboard systems, you will need to know who made the actual equipment. For example, if you see the name 'Hubbard' on any of the refrigeration parts, then give them a call and they will explain what you need to do to guarantee peak performance. Incidentally, you may well have Hubbard equipment installed as they have been providing vehicle refrigeration for over 35 years.

Reliability of the Heating and Cooling Systems.

Like anything mechanical, problems can crop up. The good news is that the technology used in both the heating and cooling systems on the majority of vans is well proven and robust. Equipment failures are not that common.

Diesel or Petrol?

Given a straight choice, diesel is preferable. The initial purchase cost of the van is higher but overall running costs are lower. Diesel engines are more suited to the life of a sandwich van – regular stops with the engine left running.

A modern diesel powered van is capable of providing a comfortable drive. The engine will be a little noisier than its petrol counterpart, but not hugely so. Diesel technology has improved a lot in the past 12 years – in terms of fuel efficiency and emissions.

Reversing a Sandwich Van

It can be a bit daunting at first. Your rear view mirror will be useless to you, because the rear is completely filled with the cargo box. In fact your van might not have a rear view mirror fitted at all, and that is certainly disconcerting at first.

With practise, you will learn to use the wing mirrors, but even then, care must always be taken because you can never see directly behind the van. Some drivers fit a camera reversing system, which consists of a camera at the back of the van transmitting a video image to a small screen in the cab. These systems are quite cheap to install and can make reversing a safer process.

Chapter Five

Sandwiches – Make or Buy

Sandwiches won't be your only stock item, but they will make up the bulk of your sales and this chapter outlines the options you have when sourcing them. The chapter on suppliers deals with the rest of your general product lines.

You have two choices open to you. Either you make your own sandwiches, or you sell someone else's.

You will have to make the decision that most suits your personal circumstances. For example, if you have a very large kitchen maybe you could make them at home. Or perhaps build a dedicated kitchen especially for the purpose. Or, you could take the approach that I did – initially buying them in, but eventually leasing an industrial unit and fitting it out as a commercial kitchen.

Equipping a kitchen, be it a leased unit or a specially built home extension, can quickly become a complex project. Fortunately, I can steer you in the right direction, having 'Been there, done that', so to speak.

Buying Sandwiches Ready Made

For most people, this offers a relatively easy way to get your sandwich round started.

The supplier, usually (but not always) a dedicated sandwich manufacturer, will have a fixed range that you can choose from. There will be no labelling or packaging issues because you are buying a ready made product. Often, the supplier will be prepared to deliver your stock to you, but unless you have adequate refrigeration, you are better off collecting the stock on a daily basis. Naturally, this means selecting a supplier who is open early – in practise the majority will be.

Sale or return

When the working day ends it's inevitable that you'll have unsold sandwiches. I have never known any sandwich round operator return to base having sold out completely. Sometimes these leftover sandwiches can be eaten by friends or family, which at least is better than binning them, but it's still a business cost.

Ideally, you need to purchase stock on a sale or return basis. What this means is that at the end of the days trading, you can return unsold sandwiches to the supplier for a refund or credit note. Some suppliers will gladly operate on this basis from day one. But they often charge a premium to offset some of their costs, which means you pay more for the sandwiches to start with.

Other suppliers won't accept returned stock at all. What you buy you keep. Once you have proven yourself as a reliable customer, they may change this stance.

Sandwich storage

If the supplier delivers stock to you, or if you are reselling unsold stock (within the sell by date of course) then those sandwiches will need to be kept in refrigerated storage – a big fridge basically.

Once you begin storing stock that is for resale, you are obliged to comply with all the health and hygiene regulations that exist for the protection of the general public. This is an important subject that gets covered later in the book. In practise, many operators would quietly store excess sandwiches at home in a separate fridge, then reuse them the next day. Naturally, any sandwiches past the sell by date simply get binned.

Why the fuss over storing a few sandwiches at home?

The rules regarding food storage and the temperatures for various food types are quite involved and detailed. This is necessary to prevent the spread of bacteria that can lead to food poisoning. In the chapter on hygiene I provide a lot of information on this subject.

The Environmental Health Department regularly inspect all premises involved with the preparation or storage of food destined for retail sale. If you store sandwiches at home for resale, your premises would need to be inspected, just like any other business. Your fridge would be examined to ensure that it was operating within the correct temperature range.

Pros and Cons of Ready Made

There are strong points in favour of buying ready made sandwiches, at least until you have established your round. But there are downsides too.

Advantages of buying ready made sandwiches

- Time saving – much quicker to buy ready made than assemble ingredients and make your own

- Sandwiches are packaged and labelled – Saves you the hassle of setting up labelling or packaging systems

- Money saving – fewer up front costs. No need to invest in equipment or ingredients.

- You can get by with no other staff members – one man operation.

- A less stressful working day. A lot of work goes into sandwich preparation. If someone else takes care of this, you are free to concentrate on the selling side of things.

- If you purchase your sandwiches from the supplier on a daily basis, without storing them at home, the hygiene regulations are much more straightforward. If you make your own sandwiches, the hygiene rules become a lot more complex.

Disadvantages of buying ready made sandwiches

- It costs more to buy a ready made sandwich than to make your own – less profit per unit.

- You might not get 'Sale or return' option. Ready made sandwiches cost more to start with, so the loss will be higher than if you had to bin sandwiches you made yourself.

- You are likely to be stuck with a more limited menu. A sandwich manufacturer needs to sell in bulk – they can't offer the flexibility of a personalised menu.

- The packaging and labelling of your products goes a long way in establishing your brand look. Using someone else's sandwiches forces you to use their labelling and packaging types.

- You have no control over the manufacturer's hygiene standards. Your entire reputation lies in the hands of someone else. If customers get ill after eating your sandwiches, they will associate your van with poor hygiene. That can be the death knell for a sandwich round business.

Strike a Deal with an Independent Sandwich Shop

I cannot recall even considering this option when I started my sandwich round, and yet it should have been an obvious choice. Plenty of sandwich shops would have been keen for me to sell their quality products from my van. Quite possibly on a, 'Sale or return', basis.

The benefits over a sandwich factory would have included a more varied and exotic menu, together with better quality and less drab sandwiches.

Equally importantly, I could have struck up a more personal relationship with the proprietor, which is always better for business.

A few thoughts

Buying ready made is certainly the easiest and quickest way to hit the ground running. It allows you to spend more time selling and building up the round, rather than getting up at 5.30am to prepare ingredients and package your own sandwiches – not to mention running around buying supplies.

There are drawbacks, but for me, it ticked a lot of the right boxes. Time saving being the most important.

I chose to use a dedicated sandwich manufacturer, basically a factory, but with hindsight, doing a deal with a gourmet sandwich shop might have been a better option.

Making and Selling Your Own Sandwiches

If you want to make the most money possible, you need to make the sandwiches you sell. Where to make them, either at home or from a commercial kitchen unit, will be covered in the next chapter. For now, we need to look at this option when compared to buying ready made.

Until you have spent some time preparing and packaging sandwiches, you won't easily appreciate the work involved. You will spend time on all of the following.

The project time factor

Planning and fitting out a kitchen area will take time. You won't be up and running within a week or two. Equipment will need to be researched and purchased. Possibly planning consent will be needed if you intend working from home.

Sourcing and purchasing supplies and ingredients

Once you have an established menu, the time you spend visiting wholesalers and supermarkets will fall, more or less, into a set pattern. But even with a set buying plan, a lot of your weekly hours will be taken up with routine purchasing.

Ingredient preparation

Your ingredients have to ready and available before you start assembling your sandwiches. You can't prepare them, 'on the fly', as you go along – you will get into a hopeless mess if you try to operate that way. This means all washing, chopping, mixing and decanting of ingredients into suitable containers must be done either the night before, or the next morning.

If your menu consists of just 12 sandwich varieties and you make a hundred sandwiches a day, you could easily spend a couple of hours on ingredient preparation and subsequent cleaning up. This does not include the actual making of the sandwiches.

Making the sandwiches

It doesn't matter how efficient and organised you are, making sandwiches takes a lot of time.

Even with all the ingredients to hand and allowing for the labelling, I used to take nearly a minute to make a sandwich and stuff it into the hinged wedge (the clear triangular sandwich box). To make a hundred would have taken 100 minutes, assuming I kept up the pace. Add the ingredient preparation time and you can see why I chose initially to buy the sandwiches in.

Labelling and packaging

Your label has to be professional and distinctive. This means hand written labels are a no-no. I deal with labelling and its importance in later sections.

The main point to note for now is that its pretty time consuming (though not technically difficult) and it's yet another item that has to be dealt with.

Hygiene regulations

Any establishment involved in the preparation and sale of food must comply with all the relevant Health and Hygiene regulations. Most of it is common sense, as I will show in a later chapter, but it's definitely time intensive and just adds to the workload.

Pros and Cons of Making Your Own Sandwiches

In addition to the time related issues already mentioned, there are a few other points you should consider (both for and against) with regards to making the sandwiches yourself.

Advantages

- You control the costs and determine the margin. This is the best way to secure the maximum profit from your sandwiches.

- The quality of the product is down to you. You are not depending on someone else to determine this. You are free to use the best ingredients you can find.

- You are in full control of the branding, labelling and choice of logo. You have full power to decide what your brand image will be.

- The range of products and the menu is decided by you. You can chop and change your offerings at will.

- Because you make the sandwiches, you have full knowledge of the hygiene conditions – unlike if you just bought the sandwiches ready made.

Disadvantages

- You will need a suitable working kitchen to prepare ingredients and the sandwiches. Fitting out this kitchen, so that it complies with the regulations, can be costly.

- It's very likely that you will need some help. Doing all the work, from preparation to selling is a lot for one person to handle.

My Take on the Matter

Of the two approaches, buying them in is the easiest and quickest way to get a regular supply. It's the way I began and

I recommend you consider this option before spending money fitting out kitchens or renting premises.

It's true that you won't make the same profit by retailing ready made sandwiches. But that disadvantage is offset by the convenience of being able to really test the market, with out the hassle of equipping a kitchen and complying with all the rules and regulations involved.

Later on, when you have solid experience of running the business and can see where it's heading, you can decide to branch out and make your own, either from a home kitchen or a rented unit.

Eventually, that's what I did. I had enough confidence in the business to take it to the next level and went hunting for premises to use as a sandwich and food preparation unit.

If you decide to start out by making your own, then you will need to fit out a commercial kitchen. There are plenty of rules and regulations to follow, but none of it is particularly complicated to understand.

The next chapter deals with this, it's relevant whether you decide to rent a unit to make your sandwiches, or fit out a kitchen at home. This is because many of the hygiene rules apply equally, irrespective of whether the kitchen is based on an industrial estate or your own home.

Chapter Six

The Kitchen Preparation Area

Where to Make Your Sandwiches

Your very first consideration should be deciding who is going to help you. There is a lot of work involved in making sandwiches, as I explained in the previous chapter. If you plan on doing all the purchasing, preparation, selling, cleaning and administration on your own, you would be well advised to think again. I am not saying it can't be done, but it would be so much easier if you could count on a family member for support.

Even if that person just arranged the supplies, or prepared your ingredients, or took care of all the paperwork, or helped out in some other useful way.

Your next consideration should be where to make the sandwiches. You have a few options.

Working From Your Home Kitchen

Many people assume that they can prepare food at their home and then sell it from their van. This can be done successfully, but you have to comply with the law before you attempt to do it – and the rules and regulations can be quite involved.

Another point to note is that some properties, mainly older ones, could have restrictions on the type of businesses that can be run from them. This could include food preparation as well. If in doubt, check with a solicitor specialising in property law.

What if I just make sandwiches at home anyway, without worrying about all the rules and regulations?

It's undoubtedly true that a percentage of sandwich round operators make their products at home, without bothering about the legal requirements.

Your home kitchen might be the most hygienic work place imaginable, but unless you are legally licensed you will struggle to get liability insurance.

If anyone ever had a problem with one of your home made products, be it food poisoning, or choking on a piece of chicken, you might find yourself in court – facing criminal prosecution. Also, without insurance cover your personal assets could be at risk if the complainant decides to sue. In this day and age, becoming a victim of a lawsuit is far from rare.

A home kitchen is not a commercial kitchen

The term 'commercial kitchen' generally refers to any kitchen used for business purposes and designed to operate at a high capacity. This description clearly doesn't fit the average home kitchen, in terms of use, or the durability of the equipment to be found in it.

Many sandwich round owners do use their home kitchens legally. This means complying with whatever requirements your local EH (Environmental Health) officer imposes. Unfortunately, modifying an existing home kitchen so that it satisfies the local EH department can be difficult. Most local councils do not recommend running a food preparation business from a home kitchen, not on a permanent basis anyway.

One way around these difficulties is to build a separate kitchen dedicated solely to serving your business. Naturally, this only works if you have suitable space available.

Industry Guide to Good Hygiene Practise

Before you do a stroke of work planning or modifying your kitchen, get a copy of 'Industry Guide to Good Hygiene Practise.' When you have read this you will have a broad understanding of what it will take to make your kitchen compliant. The guide is available from your local EHO or from the Food Standards Agency at http://www.food.gov.uk

Get the environmental health officer involved early

Your first instinct might be to avoid contacting an EHO or any other official body but there are several very good reasons why you should approach them once you have read the 'Industry Guide to Good Hygiene Practise.' and have an idea of how to modify your existing kitchen, or plan a new one.

- You have to register as a food business with your local council at least one month before you open. This means you will get a visit from an EHO regardless.
- The environmental health department of your local council are professionals and they are there to guide and help you go about things the right way.

By contacting them first, you will have shown the EHO that you are a serious and professional business person, unlikely to give them trouble in the future.

They are busy people carrying out a vital job, show them that you can be trusted and they will have more time to concentrate on other businesses and other problems.

Just as importantly, they will be happy to look at whatever plan you have and advise you of any problem areas. It is a lot easier to sort problems out at the planning stage, rather than after they have been implemented.

Making Sure Your Kitchen Passes the Inspection

Right, this is where the situation gets a little involved. Since a home kitchen is subject to the same regulations as any other food business, complying with them in a home environment can be very challenging.

This is why the majority of local councils would discourage using a home kitchen in the first place – getting a home kitchen up to scratch can be daunting. It's certainly possible, but you need to approach the project fully informed before starting on it.

Why do the local councils have such concerns about using a home kitchen?

There are rules on floors, ceilings, sinks, ventilation, windows and even doors. There are regulations about the activities that can be carried out in a food preparation area.

For example, a home kitchen might be used for feeding pets, washing clothes, or even as a smoking room – none of this is tolerated in a commercial kitchen.

Because there are so many regulations that have to be adhered to, local councils are reluctant to recommend using a home kitchen for business purposes.

My own kitchen experiences

When the time came for me to make the switch from buying sandwiches to making them, I also went through the routine of fitting out a kitchen.

Admittedly, my kitchen was planned from the ground up and not done at home either. But since the rules are the same for a home based or commercial kitchen, my experiences are relevant whether you are planning to modify your domestic kitchen, build a new one at home, or rent a unit and start with a blank canvas.

Basic Guidelines for the Floors, Walls and Ceiling

If you apply common sense in conjunction with the information in the catering guide, you and the EHO will be on the same wave length, working within the same set of rules. It is worth remembering that the EHO is there to advise and help you, he/she is not your enemy.

Floors

You have quite a few options regarding your choice of flooring. The main stipulation is that the surface must be hard wearing, easy to clean and not absorbent. Domestic vinyl surface, often found in home kitchens, is not generally considered to be suitable – it's not durable enough. Common choices of suitable floor covering would be:

- Flooring tiles, ceramic or vinyl (commercial quality)
- Vinyl safety flooring
- Cast in situ resin flooring
- Sealed and painted concrete surfaces
- Metal plate

If you are designing a new kitchen, as an extension to your house, or within a rented unit, you should also consider using 2 pack epoxy resin flooring. It's the same kind of paint used on the floors of many garages and tyre fitting shops. It's hard wearing, easy to clean and non absorbent.

If the EHO decides that your current floor covering is not suitable, you will be advised to change it. Price wise, it's probably best to avoid metal flooring (seldom used these days). Cast in situ resin flooring has a similar look to 2 pack epoxy paint, but is harder wearing and costs more.

If you choose any kind of vinyl solution, make sure you choose commercial quality only. Domestic vinyl coverings are not strong enough to last. Other floor tiles should be chosen with care, the last thing you need in the workplace is slippery tiles.

Walls

Walls must be easy to clean and in sound condition. You cannot have loose flecks of paint or plaster falling onto the food preparation areas. Cracked tiles would also be unacceptable.

As with the flooring you have a good choice of walling materials to choose from and as long as they are properly installed, any of the following would be acceptable.

- Epoxy resin and similar coatings
- Washable painted plaster
- Ceramic tiles
- Stainless steel sheeting
- PVC sheeting

The height needs to be at least 1.8 metres. The walls above this height need not be as durable but they must still be easy to clean and in sound condition. Where the floor meets the wall covering, coving should be used as this helps prevent dirt build up.

A few words on wall cladding

My original kitchen plan called for the use of ceramic tiles as this seemed to be the most suitable and easy to clean surface. The landlord had other ideas. We had promised to carry out no alterations that would prevent the unit from being returned to its original condition. Fitting wall tiles would have blatantly contravened this agreement.

Plastering the walls was out of the question, nobody we knew had the necessary skills and using an outside contractor would have cost too much. We ruled out stainless steel sheeting and resin surfaces for similar reasons. The final option was plastic wall cladding. A bit of research soon revealed that this was the most common approach for new commercial kitchens.

Initial research on wall coverings had shown that most kitchens had tiled surfaces. A mistake was made in researching old existing kitchen units instead of newer ones. If the research had been more accurate we would have seen from the start that wall cladding was the way to go.

Plastic wall sheets

Wall cladding sheets are basically PVC linings that are supplied in sizes ranging from 1.2m wide up to 3m tall, with a few options in between. Sheet thickness can vary from 2mm up to 10mm. The cladding can be attached to the walls either by gluing or by small rivets. Companies that supply the cladding can usually offer complete fixing solutions. You can secure the cladding yourself or hire a company to do it for you. If you have any kind of DIY experience, fitting wall cladding should be a relatively straightforward job.

An awkward landlord was a blessing in disguise for me, otherwise I might have gone with the ceramic tile option. Wall cladding turned out to be cheaper, easier to fit, easier to keep clean and fully compliant with the hygiene laws. I recommend you examine this option closely, it has a lot of plus points.

Ceilings

This can be one of the trickier areas to sort out. The guidelines are straightforward in that:

Ceilings and all overhead fixtures must be designed, constructed and finished to prevent the accumulation of dirt.

The ceiling must not shed particles of dirt (or indeed particles of itself) and it must be easy to clean. Further to this the ceiling must not encourage condensation or the growth of mould.

Ventilation plays a big part in reducing condensation and this is achieved with extraction systems, not usually with direct tunnels through the roof.

Ceiling surfaces

Suitable ceilings or overhead surfaces would include:

- Smooth washable painted plaster
- Direct fixed ceiling systems
- Suspended ceilings

Commercial business premises often need special ceilings to be constructed over the food preparation area – usually a pretty costly affair. A home kitchen ceiling would already be low enough to reach for easy cleaning and as long as it's in good order, you shouldn't have any problems with the EHO.

One exception might be if the EHO believes that condensation could form on your ceiling, in which case some kind of ventilation system would be needed.

Windows and Doors

Windows

Windows must be easy to clean and designed to prevent an accumulation of dirt. The sills and framework must also comply with this. If a window is in a food preparation area and is opened for ventilation then it has to be fitted with an insect proof screen. This screen must be easily removed from the windows for cleaning purposes. In general all windows in the food preparation area should be fitted with screens.

With a bit of luck, fitting a screen to your kitchen window will be all that is needed to satisfy the EHO.

Doors

Doors leading into the food preparation area should be of the free swinging type, so as to prevent hand contact. An alternative to an actual door is the door screen, loose plastic flaps that are pushed aside when pushed against. We used these in our unit and they are a lot less hassle than constantly opening and closing doors.

If you are building a new kitchen, then fitting doors that comply with the guidelines should be a fairly simple process. However, modifying an existing domestic kitchen would probably be a bit trickier – not to mention ruining the look of your décor. One of the problems of modifying a home kitchen is that it will end up being functional, rather than pretty.

Water issues – Wash Basins, Sinks and Toilet Facilities

This is where most home kitchens run into problems. The hygiene regulations are quite specific when it comes to wash basins and sinks. Complying with them will almost certainly mean altering the existing plumbing.

Hand wash basin

Most home kitchens are not fitted with a separate wash basin, but this is a major requirement of the food safety act. This basin should be equipped with hot and cold running water. You cannot use your ordinary sink for this purpose, neither can you use the bathroom basin.

The purpose of a separate basin is so that staff can wash their hands without using the main sinks or the basin provided with the toilet facilities.

Separate sinks for equipment and ingredients

You cannot use the same sink for washing ingredients and equipment. Basically, this means you need two separate sinks. If you have a dish washer installed, your local EHO might take this into account as a substitute for one of the sinks, but that is not a certainty, so count on needing two.

Sinks and wash basins should be installed with the plumbing visible, not boxed in. This makes for easier cleaning and prevents rodent infestations. All equipment that is connected to the drainage system must have adequate traps fitted.

There is one other little awkwardness to consider when planning the layout of your sinks or basins. Toilets are supposed to feed into the drainage system *after* the kitchen sinks and basins, this ensures that the flow direction is away from the kitchen area.

Naturally, your home plumbing is already installed and modifying it is something you want to avoid. Just be aware that your EHO might take an interest in this aspect of the project.

Toilet facilities

The regulations on toilet facilities are pretty straightforward. The toilet cannot open directly into the food preparation area, there has to be a separate area with good ventilation between the two.

If you are modifying your existing home kitchen, this probably won't apply to you, since most toilets don't connect to the kitchen, but if you are planning a new kitchen, it's something to be aware of.

Ventilation and Extraction

Ventilation

In the food preparation area moisture and stale air will soon build up. This is caused by heat from fridges and freezers, cookers and the general background temperature. If this air is not expelled and replaced with clean air then condensation will build up and the ambient temperature will rise.

Your main products may be sandwiches, but some of the fillings will need to be cooked by you. Bacon, sausages and chicken are the most likely candidates. The cooking process adds to the stale air and the rise in ambient temperature.

You might find that the EHO wants to see some kind of ventilation system in place. The simplest method, and the one I chose to use, was to install a couple of 12" extractor fans through the wall. There are other options, but this was cheap and perfectly adequate. Just make sure you get fans with a variable speed control, otherwise they will be spinning away at top speed even when they don't need to be.

Extraction

An extraction system is what you use to remove cooking odours and grease from your kitchen area. A typical sandwich round operator is not going to need an extraction system that would be used by a fish and chip shop or a curry house. Many rely on the ventilation fans to expel the cooking odours and the cooking extraction system is little more than a high end domestic solution.

A quick word on fridges

I cover the types of equipment you might need in your preparation area in a later section, but one point worth noting here is that the EHO will almost certainly insist that your domestic fridge is not used for storing ingredients for your business. You will need a separate fridge.

Electrical considerations

A kitchen preparation area needs a lot of sockets. Suppose you have six 240v outlets, sounds like more than enough. One for the fridge, freezer, microwave, contact grill, food mixer, bake off oven, cooker, heated warmer, another fridge to store prepared sandwiches etc. Oops, more appliances than you have sockets for and doubling up is not a particularly clever idea. For a home kitchen, call the electrician and get some advice on fitting more sockets.

If you are renting an industrial unit, you might already have three phase electricity installed and if you do, that is quite a bonus. Some of your equipment could run off that, freeing up the 240v sockets. A lot of commercial catering equipment runs off three phase power – you might not have a need for such equipment at the start, but you may do later.

Alternatives to the Home Kitchen

As you can see, it's perfectly legal to prepare food in your home kitchen for sale to the public, as long as you comply with the regulations. And that's where the problem comes in. Those regulations were meant for commercial businesses and it's not easy for a domestic kitchen to fall into line with them. It can be done, but it's not likely to be cheap or easy.

Sharing a kitchen

If you want to make your own sandwiches but cannot realistically use your home kitchen, then think about sharing someone else's. Any food establishment that operates out of business premises will have a commercial kitchen. It's unlikely that they use their preparation area 24 hours a day.

Perhaps you could strike up a deal to use their kitchen when they don't need it. Agree on a reasonable weekly or monthly fee and you have all the benefits of an equipped legal kitchen, with none of the hassle. The business owner gets paid a fee for the use of his premises and equipment when he isn't using it anyway. A win-win situation.

It's quite likely your local council could help with this. They may even have industrial units set up already which you can rent on a monthly basis, or share with other like minded individuals. It's also possible that your EHO would suggest this approach too, instead of trying to modify your domestic kitchen.

Locating Your Own Unit and Creating a Kitchen

This certainly is an alternative to a home kitchen or a shared kitchen, though I don't recommend it for beginners. There are a lot of pitfalls. However, if you have established your round and are ready to expand to the next level then it may be a sensible path to take.

Finding the right property will take time, you will need persistence and patience. It's important to view a range of properties and not sign up for the first one you see. It's unlikely the first premises you inspect will be the one that is best for you, it just doesn't happen that way.

Suitable premises

A typical premises that would be suitable for sandwich production, would be a small unit on an industrial estate.

Avoid retail shops, the rent is usually at a premium because they are in high visibility locations –the sandwich van serves as your retail outlet.

Essentially, there are five key points to consider when hunting for a potential production unit.

- Professionals you will need to consult
- Location requirements
- Leasing property
- How to find a unit
- What to look for in the unit itself

Expert Advisors You Will Need to Consult

You will need to appoint a solicitor before you get too involved in searching for property. The firm you contact must have experience of commercial property and leases.
You will also need a surveyor to inspect any premises that pass your initial investigations. The solicitor can make recommendations on this.

An appointment will be scheduled so that you can discuss your requirements. If this is your first venture into business property, the meeting will be an important one. The solicitor will explain the procedures involved in leasing or purchasing a property. The leasing process would typically go something like this.

An agent shows you a suitable rental unit, you express interest. The agent informs the landlord, who instructs his solicitor to prepare a lease. This lease is sent to your solicitor, who then arranges another meeting with you. Both of you peruse the lease and if satisfied, sign it.

That's a bit simplified, in reality there would be delays whilst legal searches are carried out, and checks are made with regards to the class usage of the property. Delays could also result if terms of the lease were found to be unsatisfactory. But essentially that's the process. Buying a commercial property is similar but takes a lot longer and involves more legal checks and searches.

Location Requirements

I have already mentioned that you don't need a retail outlet. A small production unit away from the retail sector is a better bet. You aren't looking for crowds at your unit, it's simply your production unit.

However, you will find that the established businesses will often make loyal customers, simply because you all share the same estate. It's quite likely you could do a useful trade straight from the premises, especially if you offer some kind of hot food. This is quite apart from your normal routine of selling sandwiches and related products from your van.

You can be quite flexible in your location choice. The bargains are to be had on the older estates, perhaps the ones that look a little run down or past their best. Granted, it might be nicer to have a modern gleaming building, but you don't need a public facing presence, and the lease would definitely cost more.

Leasing Premises

The majority of people will lease premises; it's by far the cheapest way of establishing the business. If you have the resources available, then an outright purchase might be a good idea, but definitely speak to a solicitor and also an accountant before doing this.

Retail shops in the right location usually increase in value. Industrial units, especially those already a bit shabby, don't automatically increase, and a variety of other factors come into play that frequently have a negative impact on their value.

Why Lease instead of buying?

Start up capital is usually limited and few can afford the luxury of owning the property they plan to trade from. Renting is the only viable alternative.

The overall costs are much lower than buying, but will still come to a substantial amount. The deposit requested by the landlord could equal three months rent.

On the other hand, it is quite common to negotiate a rent free period. This gives you a breathing space, and helps to offset the costs of shopfitting. From three to six months is not unusual. Your solicitor will make sure that the lease agreement is fair to you, but there are a couple of points to note.

FRI Lease

FRI stands for Full Repairing and Insuring. This kind of lease lays the entire responsibility for the maintenance and insurance of the property squarely on your shoulders. If the roof needs replacing after 20 months, you have to foot the bill. If the ancient water boiler packs up, you pay to replace or fix it. This has been the standard lease type for years, and it always benefits the landlord.

Admittedly, it may be possible to offset improvements you make against future rent rises, but don't take that as a given. If you sign a rental agreement for 5 years or less, then an FRI lease is not very fair to you. Hopefully your solicitor would point this out anyway, and attempt to negotiate on your behalf, but it pays to be aware.

Any potential landlord will want assurances that you can meet your rental obligations. It's very likely that you will have to produce a bank reference.

How to Find a Unit

Simply driving around a few industrial estates often throws up possibilities, it's quite likely several units will be vacant. Take a note of the contact details and make a phone call. Sometimes you might get hold of the landlord, but usually you will be dealing with an agent.

Points to remember when dealing with an agent

Commercial property is usually handled by agents and from your point of view this makes things easier generally. There are distinct advantages to using a commercial property agent:

- There will probably be a selection of empty units available, allowing for quick occupation.

- You will be able to compare several properties within a short space of time.

- You can question the agent, to find out what current rent rates are.

- Your details will be added to the agent's books, you should hear about suitable properties quickly.

Going through an agent could save you a lot of time, but be aware of the following.

- The agent is working for the landlord, not for you.

- Investigate several properties, never agree to take the first one.

- Always go back for a second and third visit, this helps to build up a more realistic impression of the property.

- Don't forget to negotiate a rent free period if at all possible.

- Verify that the rent is fair, compare it to similar properties.

Classifieds

Don't overlook the small ads, landlords often advertise directly in the hope of avoiding agents and the fees they charge. You will still have to take all the normal precautions such as having the building examined by a surveyor, but dealing directly with the landlord, you have a better chance of negotiating a rental discount.

Online searching

The internet can be useful in many areas of your business, not least because of the research opportunities it offers. There will be a lot of property online that you can investigate. One of the most useful aspects is that you can compare a range of similar properties and the rents being requested.

What to Look for in the Unit Itself

The size of your unit would not need to be any bigger than 40 square meters, and you can get by on 25 or 30 square meters if necessary. Because you are fitting out a commercial kitchen and not a retail store, you can be pretty flexible regarding the layout of the interior. It's likely you will be starting with a blank canvas, unless you are taking over an existing commercial kitchen.

Zoning and Planning Permission

Commercial property is zoned for specific use. Your local planning officer can give you guidance on the regulations in your area. Most local authorities would have no problem with you opening a sandwich production unit on an industrial estate.

If you were to install heavy duty extraction equipment and planned to operate a high output take-away type of business, they would have a few questions, even though it's not in a retail location.

Inspecting the premises

Your main job is to examine the property from all angles to gauge its suitability. Once you have chosen a suitable unit, the next step is to show an expression of interest. This is where your team of professionals comes into play.

You will have a fair idea of the general condition of the premises, but your surveyor will be the one who carries out the proper inspection and advises you accordingly. Some of the more important aspects of a property inspection will include the following.

- Condition of the roof
- Structural integrity of the building
- Condition of the wiring and electrical system
- Any environmental issues (such as asbestos removal)
- Gas boiler / heating system / plumbing condition
- Any issues with damp

A cautionary tale

Perhaps if I relate my first property experience it will help to emphasise the importance of having a full inspection carried out by you, your surveyor, or other professionals, before committing to a lease or purchase.

I was shown a small unit by a local agent. The outside was reasonable, and the inside was clean enough. The previous tenant had run a food distribution company. It had three phase power and a gas point. Walls were smooth and clean and so was the floor. After less than ten minutes I agreed to take the place.

The agent phoned the landlord who instructed his solicitor to prepare a lease with completion date set four weeks ahead. The timescale seemed reasonable and I set about planning and purchasing fittings and equipment.

After two weeks I phoned the agent, who assured me everything was on track. Three days before completion date I phoned again. This time I was told that the landlord's solicitor had mislaid the lease and was drawing up another. I was not a happy person. Within three days I was supposed to be in the unit, fitting it out.

Eventually, ten days after we were supposed to have moved in, I lost my temper. I phoned the agent and said that unless I had the keys within 24 hours the deal was off... I had the keys that afternoon, before signing the lease! Unbelievably, the landlord's solicitor still hadn't got the lease ready, this was incredible inefficiency.

To cut a long story short, I went to the unit, opened up and looked around. It soon became apparent that there were problems. The drains were blocked, and the toilet wouldn't flush properly, it was also covered in a yellow paste that looked like sawdust.

Further investigation revealed that the sewer pipe did not actually connect into the mains drainage system, the previous tenant had carried out strange modifications for unknown reasons, and the pipe now evacuated to a swampy gravel patch at the back of the unit.

Things got worse. There were letters addressed to the previous tenant, he had been running a nappy cleaning business, and not a food distribution business, as I had been led to believe. The swampy gravel area would definitely have been subject to an environmental clean up order. The premises were not suitable for food production.

I returned the keys, cancelled all negotiations, and instructed my solicitor to proceed no further with the matter. I also said a quiet prayer of thanks for the inefficiency of the landlord's solicitor.

Luckily I didn't get my fingers burned, I paid no deposit and signed no contract. If proper research had been done, I would have avoided the property altogether. I learned my lessons from this experience:

- Visit a property more than once, at least two if not three times, it's the only way to pick up on problems.
- If you insist on inspecting a property yourself, without the use of a surveyor, then inspect it properly.

- Don't just assume that the plumbing works, or indeed that there is plumbing, test it.

- Find out what the building was used for previously, otherwise you might have to pay for an environmental clean up.

- Take a torch with you when checking premises, or better still turn on the lights (yes the lights were working, no I didn't test them, preferring to stumble around in the dark).

Looking at this experience, it's very easy to see that I did everything wrong. I visited the property once, didn't turn on the lights, didn't inspect anything properly, didn't organise an independent inspection and just assumed that gas, electricity and plumbing were in working order.

If the lease had been signed and the deposit paid, it would have been disastrous.

A Few Final Thoughts

Fitting out a kitchen, either by modifying your home one, or starting from scratch in a rented unit, is a task that should be researched thoroughly – before you spend any money. If you are on a limited budget then consider striking a deal with an existing food company, as mentioned earlier.

Whichever path you choose, the process of making sandwiches and your other product lines involves equipment, and that is the subject of the next chapter.

Chapter Seven

Equipping the Kitchen

Any food preparation venture will need equipment of some sort and sandwich making is no different. Unless you are renting a fully equipped commercial kitchen, the process of choosing what to buy and where to get it, is down to you.

This is a very important part of the business and you will still have research to do even after reading this chapter, but you'll definitely have a very good idea of what you need and why.

New versus Used

This gave me a lot of trouble in the early days, buying everything new would have been perfect but quite frankly my budget did not permit this. If your budget can stretch to purchasing everything new from the word go, then you won't go far wrong

However if your finances are a little tighter, then a combination of new and used is feasible. I decided that since the kitchen equipment was not for public display, it didn't need to look shiny and new just for the sake of it. On this basis I reasoned that used equipment would be fine from a cosmetic point of view.

Domestic versus Commercial

The minute you start researching equipment, one thing is going to stand out above all else and that's the price. Commercial quality fridges, freezers, ovens etc. cost vastly more than domestic equivalents.

The reason is that they are built to withstand a lot more use and abuse than anything you are likely to find in your home. Also they tend to be larger and more powerful. You can buy a bread knife at a supermarket for £10, but a commercial quality one could cost anywhere from £35 to £90. Some of the prices are a bit frightening; they certainly scared me in the beginning.

Unfortunately, using domestic grade fridges, freezers, ovens, etc tends to be false economy, they just don't last. You may be able to use a combination of the two. For example your main ingredients fridge will get very heavy usage, but a secondary one might be utilized a lot less, or used for storing small items.

A lot of your supplies will be in bulk, even butter or cheese comes in fairy weighty volumes and the glass shelves of a domestic fridge won't last long unless mollycoddled. It's not just the heavier supplies that cause problems; it's also the constant opening and closing of the doors.

In reality, it has to be said that there is not much of a place for household appliances in a commercial production environment.

Equipment Sources

New

There is no shortage of suppliers willing to sell you everything you could ever need, and quite a lot that you may never need. Search online and you will find plenty of ordering opportunities.

Used

If you want to buy used equipment you can buy directly from merchants or from catering auctions such as Hillditch (01666 822 577 www.hilditchauctions.co.uk). Quite a few companies will deliver to you, so you don't even need to own a transit van.

EBay

EBay has proven to be a good source in the past. I have purchased a fair bit off that site and had it delivered. The one problem with buying heavy items is that most of the time you will have to collect from the seller yourself. Overall though, EBay has proven to be a very good site for purchasing and selling catering equipment.

What You Are Likely To Need

Refrigeration

Your single biggest purchases are likely to be your fridges and freezers. The prices can be anything from £500 to over £2000. As I mentioned earlier, domestic offerings are much cheaper, but a lot less durable.

How many and what type will you need?

Experience has shown me that one large chest freezer, one large double door fridge and one smaller single door fridge should prove adequate for starters. If you need more capacity you can add it when necessary. Standard fridges and freezers are supplied quickly, often by next day delivery.

If possible try and purchase new, your refrigeration equipment must be reliable at all times. If you do buy used then try to buy as close to ex-demo as possible, or at least from a supplier that has refurbished equipment for sale. Buy from auction only if the unit is sold as working, or can be seen working. Buying catering equipment at auction can definitely result in cost savings, but only if you approach the idea with your eyes wide open.

I have to confess that my first purchases were from a catering auction, both top quality brands and both running at the time. I had them delivered without any problems. I did make contact with a local refrigeration company who checked them over and gave them the all clear. Annual inspections were carried out to make sure they stayed in top condition. I would advise you to make contact with a refrigeration expert at the earliest opportunity, don't wait until you actually need one!

Fridge and freezer maintenance

As a rule, refrigeration equipment tends to be well behaved, as long as you adopt common sense practise. Watch out for dust and dirt build up in the condenser core, this is the radiator like grille that transfers heat way from the fridge unit, use a soft brush to gently clear any debris that gathers.

Get into the habit of making sure that the compressors are turning on and off at regular intervals, you can't easily check this during the working day, there is usually too much going on and too much noise. In the evening when things are a little quieter, it will be easier to tell if the fridges and freezers are cycling as they should.

If a compressor stays running constantly then it will wear out, giving you an unpleasant bill. The common cause of this happening is thermostat failure, which in itself is a relatively easy and cheap fix.

Running temperatures

Nowadays, just about all fridges and freezers will have digital or LED readouts indicating the internal temperature. Your perishable food, by law, must be at 8 degrees or lower. Set all fridges to 5 degrees, this helps compensate for the constant opening and closing. Freezers should be set to -15 degrees, this helps compensate for the frequent opening and closing.

The Oven

It's unlikely that you will sell only sandwiches. Quite possibly, you will be offering some kind of hot food, or baked treats as well. This will involve the use of an oven to some degree.

For sandwich businesses, the most common choice is known as a 'bake off' oven because it is primarily used to 'bake off' baguettes, rolls, breads, pies, pasties etc from frozen. Most bake off ovens are quite suitable for other cooking purposes as well.

The choice available is quite bewildering and the prices can be astronomical. Do a bit of research and you will discover the top brands, names like Salva and Hobart will crop up a lot, but there are many more.

The capacities of these ovens vary from single tray, up to twenty trays for full time bakeries. Your main use will probably be in heating up baguettes, rolls and frozen baked confectionaries. I would suggest a five tray oven would be more than adequate for the average sandwich round business starting out, with a tray size of 600mm X 400mm.

Oven price

New commercial ovens can cost thousands, but suitable used ones can be purchased from about £250 upwards. You might be tempted to stick with a domestic oven, at least to start with, but the limited capacity of the trays might hamper your productivity. Also, domestic ovens do not offer the same level of reliable heat transfer.

A second hand oven can make a lot of sense, it's the route I took and I suspect the majority of sandwich round operators do the same. Despite the benefits of buying a used oven, there are some factors to consider.

- Make sure it is a known brand, with spares and servicing available.
- Don't choose one with excess capacity – you pay the electricity bill!
- Try to buy reconditioned rather than second hand.
- If choosing a gas oven, get it inspected by a verified expert.
- Check the power requirements – many ovens are wired for three phase.

One final word on ovens. An average size 5 tray unit can be as much as 1m deep and weigh 100kg. Like most catering equipment, the typical commercial oven is built to last.

Heated Food Warmers

Sandwich round operators often sell hot food, such as pies or pasties, from their vans. They can only do this if the van is equipped with a food warming cabinet. You cannot easily keep food piping hot unless the warmer is an integral part of the sandwich van itself.

Generally, you would load the warmer with your products before you set off on your daily run. After 30-40 minutes of driving, the warmer cabinet will have raised the temperature of the food until it's nice and hot, at which point you can sell it.

But what if you cannot afford to wait 40 minutes until the van warmer has done its job?

If you need the hot food in a hurry, then the only option is to pre-heat it and then transfer it to the van warmer when you are ready to set off.

Strictly speaking, another option would be to load the van 40 minutes before you intend to leave and activate the warming cabinet, but since this could mean leaving the engine running on a modern van, it's not really viable. Even if the warmer is gas powered, it still wouldn't be a good idea to leave it unattended.

A simple solution would be to use a heated food warmer in the kitchen. There are two types to choose from.

- **A heated display unit** - also known as a pie warmer, is a fairly standard piece of equipment, often seen in cafes, fish and chip shops etc. It simply keeps food warm and on display. If you choose this method of warming the food, make sure it has a moisture tank fitted to prevent the food from drying out.

- **A hot food cupboard** - does not have display glass and does not sit on a counter, it usually costs significantly more than a heated display but its capacity is higher. I started out with a hot food cupboard, but I have to say it was not utilized efficiently for a long time and provided more capacity than was needed.

In theory, you could use your oven for this, but in practise it's hard to control the heat transfer and there is a risk of the food drying out.

Microwave Ovens

You have to analyse what is going to be on your menu to see what type of microwave oven you will need. The power rating you choose will be directly related to how much use you will be putting it to. I didn't need one at all at the start, so maybe you can hold back for a while and then choose.

Commercial models do have a significant cost, so if you can do without one for a while it may help ease the cash flow. If you don't anticipate doing much microwaving, then a domestic model would probably be fine.

Meat cutters

You may choose to buy a meat slicer, similar to those used by the deli counters in the supermarkets. Choose one that will be suitable for your needs, you do not need a top end expensive model. Conversely you are wasting your money buying a domestic cheapie. A hand operated one is cheaper than an electrical model and will do a surprisingly good job.

If your budget is tight, you can probably do without a meat cutter at first, but it's a very useful piece of equipment that will definitely earn its keep.

Preparation Tables

A decent length stainless steel table can cost £500 or more. Fortunately, second hand ones are not in short supply and tend to go for about £250.

Equally fortunately, if you discover you need an extra one, you can and add it to your kitchen without causing major upheavals. Looking in the catering equipment catalogues online you will see two types are available.

- Centre tables are designed for working areas away from walls, in the centre of a room for example.

- Wall tables are designed to be butted up against walls.

The only difference is that wall tables have a lip that extends the length of the table and faces the wall side. This lip is known as an upstand and is for hygiene purposes. If you use a centre table against a wall, your local EHO will make you move it.

Stainless steel is the preferred working material for all catering preparation surfaces. Whilst other materials, such as plastic may not actually be illegal, your EHO will take a dim view of it. Forget about using wood - that is definitely not acceptable because of absorption issues.

You can also use shelves bolted to the wall as preparation surfaces, as long as they have an upstand fitted which faces the wall. Portable trolleys can serve as temporary storage areas, but are not generally that good as preparation areas.

Specialist preparation tables

There is a very nice unit which makes an ideal sandwich preparation area. It consists of a standard steel table, with a selection of steel ingredient pots alongside each other, raised a little into the air for easy access. The steel pots (correctly termed as Gastronorms) are removable for easy cleaning.

There are quite a few specialised preparation tables of this nature available in the market place. Some are even refrigerated to keep the ingredients fresh for as long as possible.

Your choice of tables and preparation surfaces will depend mostly on the size and layout of your kitchen. Don't assume all tables will fit without question into your premises, make measurements first.

Sandwich Heat Sealers

The packaging of sandwiches is covered in a separate chapter, but since we are dealing with equipment, then a description of heat sealers is relevant.

For sandwiches that are to be placed in plastic wedges, you have the option of hinged wedges which are self sealing, or wedges without lids that have a plastic film melted onto them. I fully recommend using hinged wedges for your venture. Using them is simple. Make a sandwich, pop it into a plastic wedge and close the lid over it. Straightforward and adequate.

Using heat sealers and melting the film onto a wedge is definitely a more complicated task and is more suited to businesses making lots of sandwiches for other retailers to re-sell. As you get busier you can consider investing in a heat sealer but it is certainly not necessary at first.

I learned this from experience after spending a fair sum of money buying a used one on EBay. It just wasn't practical and the fumes of melting plastic were not pleasant. I put it up for sale again fairly quickly and went back to using hinged sandwich wedges.

Sinks

By law, you must have one sink for washing and preparing food and another for washing equipment. There are usually plenty of used sinks available at the catering auctions and this can lead to significant cost savings.

It has to be said that catering equipment does not always look particularly pretty, sinks are no exception. They are long steel structures with cavernous sink areas and no built in cupboards - you may get an exposed shelf or two but that is all. Sinks need to be exposed, with no doors and drawers to provide hiding places for rodents. Most of your kitchen will be exposed like this, keeping rats and mice out is a priority.

Miscellaneous Small Items

The smaller items can catch you by surprise. It's fairly easy to work out how many fridges you will need, or how many tables, but what about knives, cutlery, storage for ingredients etc. If you are not careful, the total spend on smaller items can get way out of control.

To cite a simple example, to cut a sandwich in half you will need a bread knife. You dutifully search your suppliers catalogue and discover that a suitable knife could set you back £90. If you purchase just two knives that's £180! and that's just for starters. You search a little more hoping to find some reasonably priced ingredient pots. You discover that suitable ones start at around £15 each, you may need ten or more. The costs are rising and you've hardly bought anything yet.

This situation faces everybody who is new to the sandwich business. Some people go all the way and spend whatever they think is necessary. Some can afford to because they are not financially limited.

Others spend whatever they think they should regardless of their financial situation. What a lot of people don't realise, until after the event, is that catering suppliers are there to supply the whole of the catering industry, from a small production unit to the busiest industrial kitchen.

Consider the options

A frantically busy city restaurant may need expensive stainless steel pots for holding ingredients, but do you?

Do not assume that the expensive option is the best choice for you. Always consider the alternatives.

I could have bought £90 bread knives when I started out, after all, if a sandwich business could not justify such a purchase, who could? As it turns out, I have never paid more than £25 for a good knife, you don't need to either.

Don't buy what you don't need

I have mentioned keeping the costs down when buying the small equipment that you need. But just as importantly don't lumber yourself with things that you don't need.

During your planning stage you will come up with lots of items that seem absolutely essential to your venture. In part, this list will have been created by examining other businesses and seeing what they use. The trick is to analyse the list and see if you really need it. I can best explain this with a practical example.

During the equipment planning stage for my kitchen unit, it became apparent that there was going to be a lot of tomatoes cut up for sandwiches. Research showed that a device called a Tomato Witch could slice tomatoes rapidly and evenly. This little machine was an American import and cost £225.

It seemed to be the perfect solution. However, I failed to notice that this device was intended for high capacity kitchens supplying multiple shops. It would have been complete overkill for my little venture.

Family members stopped me placing the order. Instead I purchased a tomato knife (total cost £6) which worked out fine. As it turns out, you can easily cut up enough tomatoes with a knife to keep up with demand.

I admit I got it wrong over the Tomato Witch, but it's an example of what can happen.

Keep the costs down

Cost saving has been a theme of this chapter. That's because when you start up, cash is definitely king. The less you spend, the more you have for contingencies.

Obviously there is a balance. You need equipment of a certain quality and durability, but that need must be balanced against the budget - and when it comes to purchasing equipment, the budget has a nasty habit of rising.

Keep a firm grip on the spending reins. Admittedly, gleaming sinks, or shiny new prep tables would be lovely, but old ones work just as well and you can upgrade at a later stage. Keep the costs down.

Chapter Eight

Deciding On A Menu

Not too surprisingly, sandwiches will feature prominently on your menu. A typical sandwich van will have a range of other products as well, which we will examine later in the chapter.

Sandwich Varieties

Deciding what sandwiches to include on your menu gives free reign to your creativity. You can experiment with recipes from all over the world. Naturally, this doesn't apply quite as much if you are buying ready made sandwiches from a supplier, because then you are limited to what they sell.

However, assuming that you are making your own sandwiches, then getting inspiration is quite easy. You can see what your rivals sell, simply by looking at their menu and buying a few samples. Some might be offering bland, average sandwiches (which is good because you can easily outshine their menu) whilst others may be catering to more exotic tastes. Naturally, you should also visit a variety of local sandwich shops to get an idea of what is popular.

The internet is a wonderful source of information, just about any sandwich shop that has a website also displays their menu. You can select from thousands of choices worldwide, picking up tips, ideas and recipes that you can incorporate or use to increase your range.

Exotic Tastes

I read a report not long ago that claimed peoples tastes were becoming more exotic and I can vouch for this. Customers are becoming a lot more adventurous with their choice of sandwiches.

However, I can also state with absolute certainty that many of the old favourites will have to be on your menu. Not everyone is impressed with avocado as a sandwich ingredient and you don't want customers walking away because they can't find something basic and simple to satisfy them.

Compulsory Offerings (Almost)

The British Sandwich Organisation publishes data on the most popular selling sandwiches and the results are interesting. The top fillings are:

- Unflavoured chicken
- Ham
- Tuna
- Bacon
- Flavoured chicken
- Egg
- Prawn

I would add cheese to this list. Grated cheese and pickle, or cheese and tomato are still popular sellers. And cheese comes in so many more varieties than just mild cheddar.

The research shows that a plain roast chicken sandwich is still one of the top sellers anywhere in the UK. Chicken is undoubtedly going to be one of your principle ingredients. Other sandwiches that I strongly recommend you add as part of your basic menu would be:

- **BLT**
  Bacon, lettuce and tomato with mayo.

- **Roast Chicken Salad**
  Chicken breast, lettuce and tomato, with or without mayo.

- **Tuna, Sweetcorn and Mayo**
  Easy to mix up, do not buy pre-made tuna sweetcorn mix.

- **Egg Mayo**
  Again, you can mix your own, you don't need to buy it ready made.

- **Cheese Ploughman's**
  Cheddar, smooth pickle, lettuce, tomato, mayo.

- **Cheese Ham and Tomato**
  Mild Cheddar with ham (cut ham, not wafer thin) and tomato.

- **Chicken and Bacon**
  Roast chicken with bacon, sweetcorn, lettuce and tomato.

Of course, if your van is going to specialise in selling only French or Italian style sandwiches or some other speciality, then maybe you could do without these basic offerings.

But I would bet that even then, these fillings will still make up a large part of your menu, one way or another.

Vegetarians

It is definitely a good idea to have several sandwiches on your menu suitable for vegetarians. Use clear labelling to push the point home. Also remember that not everyone likes mayonnaise, catering for this is as easy as making sure some of your standard sandwiches are free of mayo.

How Many Sandwiches Should Be On The Menu?

Even though you are running a van and not a fully fledged sandwich shop, your menu still has to look impressive. Customers expect choice and variety. Not only should you offer the basics, you ought to cater for more exotic tastes too.

Even customers devoted to their sandwich favourites will probably want a change at some point. The menu has to be exiting, new sandwiches will have to added, old ones dropped, favourites modified.

If you buy sandwiches ready made from a supplier, you can have a pretty large menu, because you don't have to make them. But if you are the maker, then it pays to be realistic. You cannot offer every option under the sun. Whilst this might seem to be a serious limitation there are two points to note.

- If you make your own, you can pick and choose and create some truly imaginative offerings – your customers will be more interested in exotic unusual sandwiches, than racks of mediocre ones.

- It's best not to offer too many options; otherwise it really does take the customer longer to decide what to buy. It's necessary to strike a balance between your sandwich range and how long the customer stands there thinking. It only takes a few static customers to really cause a log-jam.

Avoiding boredom

You cannot get complacent and just assume your menu can stay static indefinitely. Keeping the menu in a state of evolution attracts new customers who may be keen to try something different and also ensures existing ones are kept satisfied with new choices.

Boredom has to be avoided at all costs, if a regular stops visiting the van because your offerings are unexciting, it's going to be a battle winning that customer back. This does not mean chopping and changing every two minutes. Rather, you need to make sure that every couple of weeks or so there is something different about what you offer. It could be as simple as adding an exotic cheese filling to a few of the sandwiches, or maybe creating a brand new menu item.

Most people look forward to their lunch break, it's nice to browse and decide what to eat for the day. It's your job to provide quality fare, but at the same time, you need to keep them interested.

There is no set answer as to how many sandwiches should be on the menu. That will depend on the style of your business and whether you intend to specialise. Some sandwich rounds get by on as little as 15 items on a menu, others have 30 or more

My advice would be to start with the basics and add enough exotic choices until you have around 20 sandwich items. You can add more (if necessary) once you have a feel for the market.

Don't get carried away

You might think that 15-20 choices doesn't sound like much, until you start making them – that's when you realise the amount of work that goes into sandwich production. If you are buying ready made sandwiches, then you can be more flexible. But even then, as I noted earlier, don't add too many options to the menu; otherwise your customers will spend ages browsing before they buy.

It is easy to get carried away by the variety on offer, but do remember that tastes vary worldwide – don't assume that all your offerings will prove popular. Sometimes you have to experiment and see what sells – it's all part of the fun.

What Breads to Offer

The days of offering bread in two formats, brown or white, are long gone. The varieties available now are extremely varied. Where to get bread from is covered in the chapter on supplies, but to give you some idea of what you can offer, have a look at the following examples.

- Focaaci
- Ciabatta
- Stone ground rye
- Brioche
- Walnut
- Rosemary stick
- Honey loaf
- Organic
- Scofa

This is by no means a complete list and doesn't take into account that much of the above will be available in sliced, unsliced, rolls, baguettes, with seeds or without.

Gourmet sandwich breads

A lot of these breads would be found in gourmet sandwich shops (outlets that try to rise above the ordinary by offering more exotic sandwiches). There is no way you can stock this variety of breads in your van, not without major logistical problems.

However, there is nothing stopping you experimenting with a few varieties. Most sandwich van operators are still not very adventurous when it comes to bread choices. By offering something a bit special, you could find your niche and build up a regular client base.

One word of advice. When experimenting with bread types and general ingredients, be aware of nut allergies. Anything on your menu that contains nuts of any kind should be clearly labelled – better yet, avoid selling anything that contains nuts.

Sandwich types

By this, I simply mean the various ways in which a sandwich can be presented. For the sake of simplicity all of the following are referred to as sandwiches.

- **Sandwiches sold in wedge packaging** – like you see in supermarkets or petrol station forecourts.

- **Rolls or baps**

- **Baguettes or subs**

- **Chunky sandwiches** – usually wrapped in Clingfilm with a label.

You will probably sell a combination of these, rather than sticking to one format. Customers do appreciate the variety. The packaging needed will be handled in the next chapter.

Twenty Ingredients – One Hundred Sandwiches

If you have done your research and seen how many varieties some sandwich shops offer, you might be feeling a little bit panicky. It must be an awful lot of work, involving hundreds of ingredients to produce a full menu, mustn't it? After all, if a shop has fifty sandwiches listed they must have a huge operation.

A handful of ingredients

Since your van is basically a mobile sandwich shop, it would be useful to see just how a typical shop manages to produce such a menu variety.

The way that a sandwich shop offers massive variety is not by having hundreds of separate ingredients, it's by mixing and matching a limited number into a variety of sandwich combinations. Add to this the various bread, roll, or baguette options and suddenly you have more sandwich choices than you are likely to need, and all from a limited, easily manageable ingredient base.

Actually, with twenty ingredients, you could create many more than one hundred different types of sandwiches, but it proves the point.

Flexibility

This is the advantage that you have over the franchised operators. You can introduce new sandwich lines at the drop of a hat. If your latest experimental offering does not work, then you can drop it without to much fuss, and try another sandwich type. It's easy to get a bit carried away with all the options and possibilities, but you have to remember that every sandwich you prepare and sell has to be top quality. Don't sacrifice quality for the sake of variety.

Sandwich Making

When you have created your sandwich list and assuming you won't be using ready made, you need to make sure that you (and anyone helping you) can prepare each type confidently and accurately.

Be prepared to have sandwich training days, before you start selling from the van. It might seem silly to think that anyone would need training in how to make a sandwich, after all, most of us have been making and eating them at home for generations.

The fact is, to make a sandwich that looks good and has the right balance of ingredients, does take practise and some skill. Basically it comes down to experience, that's all. Don't expect to be an expert at making sandwiches until you have been doing it for a while.

The shelf life of a sandwich

Ideally a sandwich should be eaten the same day that it is made. But you only have to visit a supermarket or local café to see that sandwiches have sell by dates of up to 3 days in advance. Does it matter?

Until fairly recently, I would have scorned the quality of a sandwich purchased from a superstore or a petrol station, but I have to admit that times have changed. It is now possible to purchase a very acceptable sandwich which could have been on display for a day or so.

Should I dispose of all sandwiches at the end of the day?

Inevitably, when you start out in the business there is going to be a lot of waste, you cannot avoid that. Whilst you are building up custom, your menu has to be full and complete, regardless of the waste. You have to provide the choice and variety that your customers expect.

If you cut back on choice, or if you run out of stock too early, customers will get irritated. Do it repeatedly and you risk losing them altogether. It's important that your van looks full, empty space doesn't look good to customers.

Eventually, your waste situation will become more manageable as your customer base increases and you are left with fewer sandwiches to dispose of.

When I started out, all sandwiches that were left over on the display were either eaten by grateful friends or family members, or else they were binned. I learned to live with this and in truth the amount of waste was not that bad. I did eventually realise that sandwiches made one day, chilled, and sold the next were perfectly fine as long as the ingredients and bread were the freshest possible.

If you intend to resell sandwiches you made the day before (and let's face it, most operators do) then make sure they stay refrigerated constantly and are labelled to prevent old sandwiches accidentally being sold. The regulations on the display of food and temperature ranges are covered in the chapter on Hygiene.

I would never recommend keeping a sandwich for three days, despite what you see for sale elsewhere, the bread starts to go soft, and the ingredients lose the crisp look. In any case, a sandwich that does not sell within 48 hours should not be on the menu.

Friday sandwiches should be sold or eaten on Friday, do not keep them until Monday.

Adding to the menu

Even the most specialised sandwich van will have a variety of additional choices to tempt the customer. You can take it for granted that your competitors will have a comprehensive and tempting menu.

Nowadays the customer expects it and will probably look elsewhere if you don't provide it. Always remember though, that adding variety is pointless if you cannot back it up with quality.

Hot food

If your van is equipped with a food warming cabinet (and perhaps also a Bain Marie), then it makes sense to use it. Pies, pasties, baked potatoes (pre-cooked in your kitchen) can all be sold successfully. At one time I even sold burgers with a fair degree of success. Hot sausages and bacon rolls are always a firm favourite.

Don't assume that office workers just eat sandwiches and industrial workers prefer hot food, because in my experience hot food is popular everywhere, summer or winter.

Cakes, biscuits, patisserie, cookies, croissants

If you have the skill and the time, there is nothing to prevent you mixing and baking your own cakes or other confectionary. You could also buy in fresh cakes and keep them chilled.

Bake off ovens were mentioned in the kitchen fitting chapter. It's quite likely that you won't have time to make cakes or biscuits from scratch, but you can buy part baked or frozen dough from specialist suppliers. The results can be very good, with the added benefit that very little of your time is taken up preparing ingredients.

There are lots of new angles that a bake off oven can give you, what about a breakfast run selling croissants to people as they get to work? Or offering to bake special cookies for children's birthdays? Not to mention the seasonal possibilities. A bake off oven can expand your business beyond the initial idea of operating a sandwich round – there are a lot of possibilities for extra business.

You could build up a seriously good niche and really establish your identity by offering fresh baked goods.

Your range of drinks

Fortunately it's relatively easy to supply a good range of cold drinks. You buy them in bulk and they have a long shelf life. So there is little reason to skimp on the variety, you are not likely to have a lot of waste.

Apart from keeping the customer happy, a selection helps to give an impression of a busy, full, well stocked van. Diet drinks must also be on display, not just as an afterthought but as a good portion of your cold drink menu. The same can be said of fruit drinks.

If you have the facility to sell soup then you can expect a good profit margin, it sells quite well even in relatively warm months. Bottled water should also be on the menu.

Salad boxes / fruit boxes

Preparing salad boxes is not a difficult task, the packaging is readily available from wholesalers, complete with forks and spoons. For inspiration you can do what I did, visit the supermarkets and see what they offer.

With fruit boxes you can be quite imaginative, we are fortunate in the UK that there is no shortage of exotic fruit available for most of the year.

Vegetarian lines

You should have sandwiches already listed on the menu for vegetarians, but you can expand upon that, perhaps build a reputation as *the* place for anything and everything they could want at lunch time.

For dieters

Currently, you don't have to supply nutritional information for sandwiches which you make and sell yourself, but if you can offer the calorie content and nutritional values of your sandwiches, you may well gain the custom of people who are weight conscious. At any one time in the UK, there are a lot of people on a diet.

Crisps / sweets and other snacks

Even though you primarily sell sandwiches, which are seen as a healthy food, your customers will expect to see a range of other goodies in your van. Most of these food types have a long shelf life, so there is little risk in keeping a good selection available.

Yoghurts and dairy products

Bit of a tricky one this. These products definitely have a shelf life and yet the dairy confectionaries are very popular. I would recommend a small selection.

I always kept a few on display, just to show that I had a well stocked van with a lot of variety, but I wouldn't recommend going overboard with this type of product. Surprisingly enough, you will be asked for milk on the odd occasion, most likely when the office has run out.

Tea and coffee

Undeniably good profit makers, in the right locations and if you are set up for it. Office parks probably won't be your best customers – they get all they want at work.

The exception to this, is the specialised type of coffee van that has a proper machine installed and can offer a quality beverage. Most sandwich vans are not equipped with dedicated espresso machines though.

Keeping the menu in motion

As I have already mentioned, the menu should never be regarded as a static item. Always be on the look out for new or interesting ideas. It's especially important to keep an eye on your rivals. You don't want to be left standing if someone else spots a trend, and starts grabbing your customers as a result.

Chapter Nine

Packaging and Labelling

It is an undeniable fact that packaging is a vital part of your image. To appear professional, your entire business needs to achieve a corporate look. The packaging you use, be it bags, polystyrene cups, clear salad boxes or baguette holders all need to be high quality and imprinted with your company logo.

But I run a sandwich round, not a shop, why the big deal?

To gain an advantage over your rivals you need quality products and a professional image. High quality packaging immediately tells the customer that they are dealing with professionals, if the packaging is this good, then the food is going to be special as well.

Buying the cheapest plain packaging from the local wholesaler is not an option if you want to project the right image. It's true that you aren't running a high street shop, but your van *is* your shop – and you need to look as professional as possible.

Your Packaging is Your Image

Even if you make the best sandwiches, bake the tastiest cookies or have the freshest baguettes for miles around, you will struggle to convince the public unless the packaging looks impressive. This is a sad reflection on modern life, where image seems to be more important than the actual product. But that's the way it is and you have to go along with it.

I mentioned in an earlier chapter that image is not a substitute for quality. If you sell shoddy sandwiches in fancy packaging, the public won't be fooled for long. You need quality combined with image.

When we started baking cakes and cookies for sale from our mobile van we knew we had a good product range, the recipes were carefully chosen and the ingredients were top quality, no added preservatives or colourings. They were sold on the basis of being 'Home Baked' rather than shop produced.

Within a week or two we realized something was wrong. Sales were disappointing. People were complaining that the range looked home made!

The packaging we had chosen was basic and the label was hand written – therein lay the problem. Customers loved the idea of wholesome home baked products, but only if the packaging was glossy and professional looking.

The public wants it both ways. They have come to expect high quality wholesome food, presented in a nice glossy package.

Sandwich Wedges

This is probably the most common form of sandwich packaging in use. You will have seen plastic sandwich wedges in every supermarket in the land, as well as at most petrol station forecourts. There are two varieties of wedge.

One type is supplied with its own hinged lid, which you push down to seal the sandwich inside. The other type of wedge does not come with a lid at all. You have to buy a special heat sealing machine and melt a thin film lid onto the plastic edges of the wedge. Stick to hinged wedges; you don't need the aggravation and hassle of a heat sealing machine. The cost of the equipment can be substantial too.

Wedge colours and sizes

Wedges are supplied in two ways. Some manufacturers give the actual sizes, so that you can judge their suitability. Others just give descriptions such as 'Deepfill' or 'Widefill' or the completely misleading 'Standard'.

You should purchase your wedges based on size rather than description, it's the only way of being sure that the packaging will be suitable.

I did my research, made the correct measurements, chose suitable bread and still got it wrong the first time. We decided to offer a Deepfill sandwich, made using thick cut bread and a Regular sandwich using medium sliced. There were various bread options, such as stone ground and granary, but all fell into the thick cut or medium category. Two boxes of wedges were ordered, one suitable for Deepfill sandwiches and the other for thinner sandwiches.

There was no problem with the Deepfills, even when the fillings were stuffed the wedge took it easily. However, the smaller wedges proved a nightmare, I could barely squeeze the thinnest of sandwiches into the wretched things, they were practically useless, a carton of a thousand wedges.

Ordering the next size up was the only option. To this day, I don't really know how I got it wrong, but two things stand out clearly.

- Do your measurements carefully the first time.
- Don't order a full box of a thousand wedges; order a few samples at first.

You can purchase wedges in a variety of colours, which certainly gives your sandwiches a distinctive look. But the cost rises substantially once you deviate from the standard clear plastic type. Most catering companies stock wedges, and there are numerous suppliers to be found online too.

I always use the standard clear wedge, rather than spending extra on fancy colours, but to make up for this my labelling is always top notch. The desired image is reached but at a lower cost. A top quality label is a darn sight cheaper than an upgraded sandwich wedge.

Wedge problems

Put simply, if you make a sandwich it has to fit into the wedge. Rather obvious, I know, but it's very easy to miscalculate. You have to give careful thought to the thickness of the bread you will be offering. Otherwise you may find yourself trying to stuff sandwiches into wedges that just don't fit properly. This will result in wedges that bulge, lids that won't close, and sandwiches that look squashed.

Avoiding squashed wedges

The best way to avoid problems is to decide what breads you want for your packaged sandwiches, and then find suitably sized wedges for them.

Everyone who makes sandwiches for packaging into wedges struggles at first, it can be frustrating, but it just takes practise. After a little while you will get the hang of it.

Buying sandwiches from a supermarket and pulling them apart will give you a good idea of how to position your ingredients. You can also pick up pointers as to the quantity of ingredients you should be using for each sandwich.

You may decide to avoid using wedges completely. But do bear in mind that a row of sandwich wedges in the van does look very neat and provides uniformity – not to mention protection for the sandwiches inside.

Film Fronted Bags

This form of packaging has a "window" at the front which allows the contents of the bag to be displayed. Cakes, cookies, bagels and sandwiches can be sealed inside. Baguette sized bags are available for your torpedo creations. Various sizes are available in varying degrees of quality.

Be sure to use film fronted bags of a good quality suitable for their intended purpose. We once ordered a batch of film fronted baguette bags, nicely printed with our logo, and proceeded to use them. We soon hit a snag with our tuna, sweetcorn and mayo baguettes.

After a while in the van's display fridge, the fillings started to make the paper bag soggy and extremely unappetising. This made the bags useless for any fillings that were potentially a bit messy. We did not want to dispose of the bags, after all they were pre-printed and we had 1000 of them.

The solution was simple; we wrapped the baguettes in cling film and then bagged them. This was acceptable temporarily. Eventually we started using rigid clear plastic packaging specially designed for baguettes.

Packaging for Other Products

You will be selling more than just sandwiches from your van , salads, cakes, cookies, bagels and the like will all need packaging of one sort or another. The thing to remember is that buying the cheapest available tends to be false economy.

If you are preparing sandwiches daily for the van's display fridge, the last thing you need are sandwich wedges with lids that won't close properly, or salad boxes that don't seal. It leads to frustration and waste.

Labelling

You need to ensure that your products are clearly labelled. The customer must not be left guessing as to the ingredients.

You don't have to list the nutritional values for sandwiches which you make and sell on your premises (your mobile van counts as your premises). However, it's sensible to make sure your customers know what they are buying before they start eating it.

For example, your sandwich label may be "Roast Chicken Salad" and underneath a brief description might say something like *"Roast Chicken Breast, with Lettuce and Cherry Tomatoes"*. If your customer later realises that mayonnaise and pepper are also on the sandwich, he/she may be aggrieved.

Always list the ingredients in the description, don't just assume that everyone knows that a chicken salad sandwich will always have mayonnaise.

If you make sandwiches that other businesses are going to sell on, then labelling requirements get a lot stricter.

Labelling and the law

If you make sandwiches for trade customers, perhaps you supply a local shop for example, then the packaging has to be labelled according to the QUID regulations. These state that the ingredients and quantities in percentage terms have to listed on the packaging. Look at any sandwich in a superstore and there will be a separate label detailing ingredients, percentages and nutritional breakdown. The exception to this might be if the sandwich was made on the premises and not supplied by a third party.

Labelling food as organic

You might be using free range organic eggs in your egg mayo mix, but that does not mean you can label the sandwich as organic. In fact you cannot even advertise that *some* of the ingredients are organic.

The laws on organic labelling are strict. If you want the right to advertise your egg mayo sandwich as having organic ingredients then you have to register and be audited. You can find more information on that by contacting ACOS (Advisory Committee on Organic Standards) http://www.defra.gov.uk

Perhaps if you are considering the idea of a purely organic sandwich menu, which could be a good niche market, there might be a case for registering and being audited. If not, then the expense and hassle is probably not worth it.

Getting the right look

As with everything else in the business, your labelling must project a wholesome professional image. There are quite a few options that you can take, some are cheap and some are horribly expensive. Practical experience has shown me that the labelling side of the business can take up a lot of your time and result in a lot of unexpected expense.

Considerations

You may be tempted to think that buying a few labels is a simple, easy and cheap process, probably not worth spending too much time worrying about. Unfortunately there are many ways you can go astray with this aspect of your venture.

For example, who will design the label? How many label types will you need for all the various items on your menu? What sort of materials will the label be made from? What about the minimum order? What about if you want to change or add products to the menu? What if you want to raise the price, but have thousands of labels pre-printed with the old price?

Thorough research

These are all questions that I had to research thoroughly and exhaustively before deciding on the best approach. I firmly believe that my final choice offers the best all round solution and is suitable for most sandwich round businesses.

You may still wish to do a little research of your own to verify my findings and experiences, but you certainly won't need to spend the time that I did, or waste unnecessary money. I will detail the various options available to you, as well as the reasons for and against their use.

Label Production – The Choices Open to You

Handwritten

You buy sheets of A4 adhesive labels and write your details and prices on them then stick these onto your sandwich wedges, salad boxes etc. Hopefully you can see that this would be image suicide. Quite apart from looking tacky, you would spend an awfully long time writing out labels for your products.

Printing Your Own Designs onto Standard A4 Labels.

You could buy sheets of A4 labels, design a suitable template and print them out on your laser printer. These standard labels can be purchased in many colours. At first glance this does not seem like a bad idea, and it's certainly cheap.

This is the route that I experimented with in the very beginning. I spent a long time designing a label template that looked halfway decent and an equally long time trying to find 'standard' labels of a suitable size to print on.

Eventually I had to order sheets of A4 labels in a custom size and then locate software that would allow me to print them out. The software was quite fiddly to use but just about manageable. I printed off the first batch, standard issue BLT (Bacon, Lettuce, and Tomato). The labels were clear, easy to read and tidy looking.

Unfortunately, they looked exactly what they were - laser printed adhesive labels. They just didn't look professional.

Added to this was the difficulty in creating and modifying templates for all the different items on the menu. It had taken ages to create just one label type. This was not going to be a quick or practical method of label production.

Ordering Labels from the Printers.

Design a label and get the printers to print you boxes of labels for all the different sandwiches and other products in your range. Seems pretty foolproof, but a couple of major issues to contend with:

Minimum print run

Normally you have to agree to a minimum print run, which could be anything from 3000 to 5000 labels. The trouble is that the print run would be for one label design only. I discovered this when requesting a quote.

Naively I assumed that the print run would consist of 3000 labels made up of our entire range. For example, I thought I could have 300 labels for cheese and tomato sandwiches, another 300 for beef and onion, and so on. It turns out that the print run was to be for one sandwich type only. So I could have 3000 labels for cheese sandwiches, or 3000 labels for beef and onion, but not a combination.

To print our entire menu range would have cost vastly more than anticipated. Granted, the look would have been professional and high quality, but the cost factor was way too high.

Lack of flexibility

Once your boxes of labels are printed, you are stuck with them. You cannot change a price, or correct a spelling error unless you cross it out and correct it by hand using a pen.

What if you decide to drop a menu item due to lack of sales? What happens to all those spare labels? You cannot use them for anything else, so they just become a wasteful expense.

Using the services of a printer can give top quality results, but it's expensive and inflexible. Also, you are still left with the problem of actually designing a nice label to start with.

Buying a Dedicated Label Printer

There are printing companies that can supply special printers designed to work with rolls of labels (unlike a standard PC printer that works with A4 sheets) So what , you might think, what's the difference between that and just printing your own A4 sheets with your own laser printer ?

Well, the big difference is that these companies do not just supply blank rolls of labels, they also offer rolls of pre printed labels with a variety of nice images and pictures.

You don't have to design any art work, that's all been done for you. All you have to do is choose a pretty label that would look good on your sandwich wedges or salad boxes.

You then use special software that is provided with the printer to input the actual description, price and other details that you require on your label.

You can save your work, update, change or delete any information you wish. There are three major advantages to producing labels using this method.

No design skills needed

You are using pre-printed labels that someone else has already designed; all you are doing is adding your details and running the labels through your printer. You don't need to do any art work or actual design.

Total flexibility

You can add or modify information easily, you can delete sandwiches from the menu or create new ones. The software available for dedicated label printers makes this task very easy.

Short print runs

Finally, most importantly, your label print runs can be as long or as short as required. You can print out 20 labels or a 100. If you print 50 labels for a certain experimental sandwich and realise it is not selling, you won't have lost much money on the labels.

Package cost

At the time of writing, a good quality printer package, with software and labels can be had for about £600. The system is staggeringly cheap and extremely flexible when compared to traditional printing.

Admittedly, you will have to carry out the task of inputting the data for your menu, doing the actual printing, as well as updating and changing products as and when necessary. This is a small price to pay considering the dual benefits of cost saving and flexibility.

The printers can take different label sizes, so they're suitable for labelling pretty much all of your menu range.

The Planglow System

Planglow is the name of a company that specialises in designing and creating labels for the food industry. They produce sheets of A4 labels with pre printed designs and images, with space on the label for you to add your own details. You use their software to add information that you want, then you print out on your own laser printer.

Have a look at their website (www.planglow.com) to see their products. The labels range from simple matt right up to glossy photo finish effect – all of them are effective and professionally printed.

Versatile

Because they specialise in the food industry, they are fully aware of the legal requirements regarding ingredients listings and nutritional values, the software provides easy to use templates for you to work with if you need to comply with the Quantitative Ingredient Declarations (QUID) rules.

It's a versatile system in that you can print a single A4 sheet of labels at a time. The system offers the same level of versatility as that of a dedicated label printer.

Until I heard of Planglow, I was all set to order a dedicated printer and rolls of labels and that would have been perfectly fine. However, I chose this company because the range they offer is stunning and the total price for four boxes of labels, each a different design, with the software, came to only £300.

I am sure there must be other companies similar to Planglow offering the same service, but I chose to go with their system and have not regretted it.

Labels as sealers

When a sandwich wedge is closed, it will need a label that covers the sealing edges, otherwise it may pop open again under the pressure of the sandwich. This is just the nature of wedges.

There are two solutions to this. You can use labels that fold over the top of the wedge, sealing it tightly. Or you can use tiny additional labels to seal the edge. Planglow cater for both types, some labels are designed to be folded over. Other sheets of labels have helper labels on the sheet that can be peeled off and used as sealers. Naturally, your other packaging can be sealed in the same way.

To Buy a Dedicated Label Printer Or Not?

I chose to use the Planglow system – I liked the idea of using a standard PC laser printer rather than a specialist label printer. Both options offer a professional, flexible approach to labelling your menu items cost effectively and easily.

Chapter Ten

Purchasing Your Supplies

Life in the sandwich business would be so much easier if you could order everything you needed from one or two sources. Unfortunately, the reality is that you could have twenty or more suppliers that you use, with varying degrees of regularity.

The Creation of a Sandwich

Let's take a realistic and practical example. As part of your sandwich stock, you prepare a Deepfill Triple Cheese Ploughman's.

Your first step might be to *butter* the *bread*, then layer one with *mayonnaise,* and the other with *smooth pickle.* You arrange slices of *cheddar* followed by *Red Leicester* and *crumbly Stilton.* Freshly cut *tomato* and *lettuce,* topped off with a sprinkling of *sea salt, black pepper* and *basil* provide the finishing touches. You place the Ploughman's into a plastic *sandwich wedge,* which has an eye-catching pre-printed *label* attached to it.

To make this one sandwich could involve up to ten or more separate suppliers. Don't assume your tomatoes and lettuce will come from the same source, or that all your cheeses can be purchased from one outlet. Choosing suppliers is a matter of balancing cost, quality and convenience. Your cheddar supplier might have the best prices for miles around, but his Red Leicester might always be out of stock.

Dealing with Suppliers

Naturally, the fewer suppliers you have the easier it is. But don't whittle your supplier choices down simply on the basis of convenience. If you try and get everything from one or two outlets, without judging the differences between them, it will cost you more in terms of price and probably quality.

Trail and Error

How are you going to determine if a supplier is a good choice for you? The only way is by trial and error. There are plenty of specialist suppliers out there, and they are keen to have you as a customer. Use this to your advantage, get free samples, negotiate a good discount structure.

Usually, the more you spend, the higher the discount you can expect. One thing is certain, if you don't ask for a better price deal, you are highly unlikely to be offered one.

When you first start out it can be quite daunting to negotiate discounts and better terms. You may not feel fully confident or competent to do so. In the UK, people often seem to be uncomfortable with the idea of haggling over the price, asking almost apologetically for discounts.

Companies will send you glossy brochures and price lists. Don't assume (as I first did) that those prices are fixed just because they are on a printed sheet. Suppliers will rarely include details of discount structures when they send out price lists, you have to ask them. Even a reduction of 5 or 10 percent on the list price is worth having.

During the early days of your business, you will be experimenting with lots of different supply companies. Don't be surprised if your supplier listing looks very different six months on. This is quite normal because it does take time to evaluate and compare your options. Existing suppliers may be dropped and new ones added. Eventually you will arrive at a selected group that meets your needs and you won't be chopping and changing every month, trying to get the best price or delivery terms.

Supplier standards

There are a couple of points to note here. If the suppliers standards start slipping, don't just put up with it, make a call to the customer service team and get it sorted. You have enough to deal with as it is, you don't need additional frustrations caused by late deliveries or unfilled orders.

Secondly, beware of any supplier that won't allow you collect an order in person or at least visit the premises. Even the large national companies (with few exceptions) delivering country wide, allow collection from their premises. Any small supplier should certainly have no problem with you visiting, unless they are hiding something.

Always remember, the quality of your sandwiches and food products is your responsibility. The health of your customers and your reputation can be damaged if you don't take care when choosing suppliers. Only choose those who are established and have a proven track record.

From The Cash and Carry to Online Ordering

Your business will bring you into contact with a variety of different supplier types, from wholesalers to specialist catering companies. Building up a list of trusted regulars is how you establish your supplier base.

Buying at the Cash And Carry

Your first visit to a wholesaler is going to be something of an eye opener. You will recognise many of the brands, but the sizes they are sold in will bear little resemblance to supermarket offerings. You will be able to purchase crisps, sweets, sauces, biscuits, cakes and much more, all in trade sized packs.

The little jar of mayonnaise that you keep at home will seem tiny compared to the 10 litre bucket you can buy at the wholesaler. Golden Syrup sold in 5 litre plastic pots, or bottles of pickle that would last the average household a decade, are an impressive first sight.

It makes sense though. When your business is off the ground, you will appreciate these bulk quantities. Imagine trying to store twenty glass mayonnaise jars in your preparation area. Every two minutes you would need to open a new one and dispose of the glass bottle - far easier to work with large plastic buckets of the stuff. It's for convenience and ease of use that you will buy many of your supplies in catering sized packs.

Try out several wholesalers

Cash and Carry wholesalers fall into two groups - those that are part of a chain and those that are independents. Don't assume that a big name wholesaler is going to automatically have better prices. Some of the smaller ones could surprise you with their stock range and pricing structure.

For some reason a wholesaler in our town always carries a far wider range of milk drinks than any of the big chains and his prices compare very favourably. Maybe it's a useful marketing ploy by the owner, because invariably I end up purchasing more than just milk drinks from him.

Even though they are referred to as cash and carries, most will take debit cards these days.

Trade only

Wholesalers are usually strict about allowing only trade customers to shop with them, the general public is excluded.

Before you can make any purchase, you have to prove that you are a trader of some kind. Then you are issued with a membership card which has to be displayed when you enter the premises. Your VAT number or a copy of your van lease would be proof that you are indeed a business. There are plenty of other ways to prove that you are eligible.

Wholesalers do want your custom, but they do their best to make sure that the general public are kept out.

Supermarkets

If you have taken the time to visit and join a wholesaler or two, you might be wondering what use a supermarket would be. Not all of your supplies need to be purchased in bulk, in which case it makes sense to save money and buy smaller quantities. Often supermarkets have specials on, such as 'Buy One Get One Free' and these can lead to worthwhile savings.

Some of your menu items might call for vegetables or fruits that don't have a long shelf life, buying locally from a nearby store could offer better freshness than having the supplies delivered.

Catering Supply Companies

These differ from general wholesalers in that the products they sell are aimed at the food and catering industry, as opposed to the general trader. Anyone who is engaged in any form of outside catering will be purchasing from them. Restaurants, sandwich bars, take aways and fish and chip shops use them extensively – and it's quite likely that you will too.

Frozen supplies

You might be surprised to learn just how much stock is supplied frozen. Everything from bread baguettes to cakes, pies, muffins and confectionary treats are all kept in deep freezers.

No matter how fresh you intend your sandwiches, pies, cakes, or cookies to be, there will be plenty of occasions when you buy frozen stock. Any company that provides outside catering makes use of frozen products. The same is true of just about anyone involved in selling prepared food to the public. There are several points to note here:

- Without the use of frozen food, the sandwich and catering industry would probably not exist as we know it.

- Keeping food frozen until it is needed is far better than having it on display in case it is needed. This equates to less waste and better hygiene practise.

- Most of the time, you wouldn't be able to tell if a baguette came from frozen stock, or was baked 5 hours ago.

It's quite probable that you'll use several catering supply specialists. Unfortunately, even though most of them offer a good range, none are likely to supply everything that you need.

Manufacturer's agents

Manufacturers often appoint agents to sell their products exclusively. For example, a pastie maker might not sell his goods to the large catering supply companies, preferring instead to use agents. These agents would typically have medium sized premises with extensive refrigeration facilities, and would probably stock the lines from a handful of manufacturers only.

These agents tend to be very generous handing out samples of their products. Pie makers seem to be especially generous, often handing out full boxes. Naturally you will need to taste these offerings, inevitably leading to cries of, 'Who ate all the pies?' You learn to live with it.

We had so many free samples at one time, there was no room in the freezers for our normal stock range, and there are only so many pies you can taste yourself.

Small specialist companies that generally act as agents for manufacturers tend to be the ones that you can establish very good relationships with. Locating these suppliers is easy – search online or look in the 'Yellow Pages' under catering suppliers.

Online Ordering

This is an area that is growing rapidly and could have benefits for your business, in that you can choose what time to place an order, even after hours if necessary. If one of your chosen suppliers has an online ordering facility in addition to the normal methods, then it's worth considering.

However, be careful of ordering supplies from companies that only offer online ordering. Remember the first rule of choosing any supplier is making sure they are reputable with a track record.

Buying Bread

In the chapter on choosing your menu, I mentioned that the varieties of bread you could keep were vast. Choosing the types of breads you would like to offer is one thing, finding good suppliers is quite another.

Even though you are running a sandwich van, you still have to offer a variety of bread choices. Not to the same degree as a retail sandwich shop, but more than the basic offering of white sliced.

If you offer unremarkable bread, which lacks flavour, your customers will have little incentive to stay with you.

Buying From a Local Independent Baker

In an ideal world you would have freshly baked bread delivered to your door, by a master baker. There are a few problems however. The independent baker is becoming something of a rarity. If you have one close to you and can reach some kind of agreement, then you really are quite lucky. Unfortunately, the reality is that in many cases you won't be buying anything from a local baker.

Dealing With a Large Bakery

The large bakeries don't just sell to supermarkets; they also sell and deliver to small companies as well. Each region will have a sales representative that deals only with the smaller clients. Generally, you would give them a call and discuss your requirements.

You might be a little surprised to find your cost price is the same as the retail price in the supermarket. You are not going to get the same discount structure as a national chain. What you do get is the convenience of regular visits with regular stock lines. That's a lot easier than running around the supermarket on a daily basis trying to find bread with a distant sell by date.

The other fact that might surprise you is the variety on offer from some of the large bakeries, they don't only bake white or brown in wholemeal or granary anymore, the range tends to be a lot more impressive.

Buying From Specialist Suppliers

There are companies that specialise in supplying bread in part baked, fully baked or uncooked form. Rolls, baguettes, baps, Ciabattas and a host of more exotic types are available in this manner.

The products are supplied frozen and you finish the baking process in your own bake off oven. Bread that is supplied fully baked just needs to defrosted and then it can be used.

Frozen breads can offer flexibility

The big advantage with these suppliers is the sheer variety they can offer. Because it is supplied frozen, you don't have to use all the bread in one go, just defrost what you need each day. The flexibility of frozen breads allows you to expand your menu without exerting any effort. You can offer just about any bread type you choose – bearing in mind the logistical issues. Bread is bulky and storing it takes up a lot of refrigeration space.

It's worth noting that in addition to specialist frozen bread suppliers, most catering supply companies will also stock a range of deep frozen bread products.

Most sandwich based businesses buy at least some of their bread in this frozen state, it's really an important option to consider if you want to offer a full bread menu to the customer. If you can't find a local supplier for some of your more interesting bread ideas, then buying frozen might be the only option.

The same companies that supply the bread products usually have a range of frozen cakes, cookies and pastries. They can also supply frozen dough should you wish to mould your own shapes.

Frozen does not mean inferior

It's important to remember that bread baked from frozen is not an inferior product, you are merely finishing the baking process, and the end result is freshly baked bread.

If you have left over bread at the end of the working day, do not re-freeze it, just throw it away and start fresh the next day with a lesser quantity if necessary.

Supermarket Bread

It's highly unlikely that your suppliers will be able to match the price of supermarket bread – they offer convenience rather than the lowest possible price.

But the range of breads available at supermarkets is impressive and in the early stages of your business, you will probably buy from them – I certainly did. However, there are a few points to consider:

Consistent supplies

For sandwiches that go into wedges, you will need consistent supplies of the same type of bread each time, to ensure the same slice thickness; otherwise you may have problems fitting the sandwiches into the wedges.

There is nothing more frustrating than trying to stuff a sandwich into a wedge and discovering that the slices are just too thick. Unfortunately, supermarkets don't guarantee to have regular stocks of exactly the same type of bread each day – this can cause you a lot of inconvenience.

Sell by dates

The other difficulty with purchasing your bread from supermarkets is that you will spend a lot of time scrabbling around the shelves trying to find bread with the longest sell by date. This might sound trivial, but it's surprisingly time consuming.

The packers put the freshest bread at the back of the shelves and you have to rake around pulling other loaves out of the way to reach them. When you need a lot of loaves, this can be quite a pain.

Cheese – Much More Than Just Mild Cheddar

Some time in the nineteen eighties, the famous writer and food critic, Egon Ronay, described British cheeses as, 'awful, ugly blocks better suited to a building site'. A lot of people agreed with him.

Happily, if this was once true, it certainly isn't now. Suppliers are starting to offer a far better range of cheeses than ever before, and this includes British cheeses. Finding suppliers is as easy as looking in the yellow pages or searching online, the same as for any other supplier.

A lot of cheese is supplied in big blocks; I always cut it up into more manageable pieces, wrap it in Clingfilm and store it in the fridge. Don't be tempted to deepfreeze cheese, I know some establishments do, but I don't believe that it's a suitable storage option.

Customers no longer accept mild Cheddar as the only option on the menu. You can't be expected to stock all varieties available, any more than you can keep every variety of bread, but you have to offer at least three types if you want to be seen as better than average. I am not knocking traditional mild Cheddar; you should still have it available as an option.

Meat, Fish and Poultry

Chicken, turkey, bacon, sausages, tuna and salmon are some of the supplies you might need. Any of your large suppliers would sell any, or all of these.

You also have the option of using independent butchers and fishmongers. There are some products that are best purchased fresh from a local supplier, conversely there are times when buying from a large wholesaler makes more sense. Chicken and tuna provide good examples.

Chicken

You can buy bags of cooked frozen chicken pieces from large catering supply companies. They are supplied sliced and only need de-frosting before they can be used as a sandwich filling. They are used extensively by the sandwich and catering trade. This seems to be an acceptable filling for an adequate chicken sandwich; the taste will be reasonable but certainly nothing special.

I personally don't use frozen chicken pieces, only breasts that we cook ourselves and cut up. I think chicken should be purchased from a butcher and cooked by you to provide the best tasting sandwich filling.

Tuna

Tuna should be purchased from a large wholesaler. One of the most popular sandwiches is tuna, sweetcorn and mayo. The tuna will invariably be of the tinned variety and will taste perfectly fine. It's just not necessary to try and buy fresh tuna from a fishmonger, it's highly unlikely that anyone could ever tell the difference between fresh and tinned, especially once it is mixed with the mayonnaise.

Eggs

Eggs are likely to feature in your business. Egg mayonnaise is one use; the all day breakfast sandwich is another. Finding suppliers of eggs is not really an issue, there are plenty.

You have the choice of battery, free range or organic. I buy free range eggs, and only from sources that don't add colour enhancers to the chicken feed. A lot of egg farmers still do this, with the aim of improving egg yolk colour.

What About All Those Exotic Sandwich Fillings?

Over the past ten years or so, exotic sandwiches have appeared with tantalizing fillings such as Cajun Chicken, Tikka, Crayfish and Rocket, Thai Prawn and Mayonnaise, Chicken Caesar and loads more. If you want to offer these on your menu, then you have two choices, make them or buy the fillings ready made.

Making your own fillings

Purists would argue that the best fillings are those with the freshest ingredients made on a daily basis. You will certainly find plenty of helpful recipes on the internet for Cajun Chicken or anything else you wish to offer.

The downside of course, is that you will spend a lot of time preparing the ingredients. Generally, fillings that you make yourself will be a healthier option because you won't be loading it with additives or colour enhancers. Realistically, making your own fillings is only feasible if you have a helping hand.

Buying ready made sandwich fillings

There are plenty of companies willing to sell you pre-prepared sandwich fillings. I can't deny that they save an awful lot of time. It's an easy way to boost your sandwich menu with no effort at all.

Butter the bread, ladle on the filling, seal the packaging and on to the next sandwich.

You won't be too surprised to learn that many sandwich businesses use pre-prepared fillings in one way or another, the time savings are hard to ignore.

There are a few disadvantages to buying in your fillings ready made. For one thing, they will be heavily loaded with preservatives, antioxidants and a host of other additives, which may not sit well with the healthy image of your business. Secondly, there is the argument that some customers might detect the processed nature of these fillings.

Supermarket fillings

Whilst I am no great fan of pre-prepared fillings, no matter how exotic, I will admit that they do have their place. It must also be said that the quality on offer has improved markedly, and that's fairly easy to prove.

Visit some of the larger supermarkets and you will notice that most of them have increased the range of sandwich fillings that they offer. They come in clear plastic tubs and are quite expensive for the small quantity you get. The idea is that you buy these fillings, take them home and prepare great tasting sandwiches with a fantastic variety of flavours. I have tasted a lot of these fillings and to be fair, they are not at all bad.

The little pots of sandwich fillings available in supermarkets can make useful testers when you want to experiment with new sandwich offerings, but don't want the expense of a full sized catering pack.

Some Final Points on Suppliers.

It's vital that your supplier base is efficient and geared towards your needs. It's equally important that you keep a firm grip on the costs.

If a supplier raises prices dramatically, try to find out why. Occasionally this will mean dropping one supplier in favour of another. Do remember though that building good supplier relationships is important for a small business, don't chop and change just to save a few pence here and there.

Chapter Eleven

Hygiene Regulations

Rules for everyone

This chapter mostly concerns those who intend to make their own sandwiches and other food for retail, rather than re-selling someone else's.

However, even then, there are rules that must be adhered to, such as temperature control, so you should read this chapter regardless.

The Rules of Hygiene

You won't be surprised to learn that the rules governing hygiene could fill an entire book. They do. However, even though the regulations are comprehensive and must be adhered to, the good news is that it mostly boils down to applying common sense.

The rules of hygiene cover every aspect of your operation. The requirements for the actual building itself, such as flooring, walling or how many sinks you should have, are all covered in an earlier chapter. Now I will focus more on staff training and food safety.

Industry Guide to Good Hygiene Practise

Before you sell a single sandwich, you should purchase the 'Industry Guide to Good Hygiene Practise.' It's available from the Food Standards Agency (http://www.food.gov.uk) or your local environmental health officer (EHO).

It's very easy to read and is broken down into sensible sections for easy digestion. I will outline the more pertinent aspects to give you some idea of what you will be required to know, in order to comply with the law when preparing food for sale.

Food Temperatures

Chilled food must be stored at a temperature of 8 degrees C or lower, this refers to the food itself, not the air surrounding it in your fridge. It is recommended that your fridges are set to 5 degrees C to allow for a margin of error. Sandwiches definitely qualify as food that should be chilled. The regulations give suggestions as to which foodstuffs are likely to be subject to temperature control, some of which include fish, egg products, and cured meats which degrade under ambient conditions.

The chiller cabinet in your van must comply with the temperature regulations as well.

Keep a record

It's a good idea to carry out daily checks on the temperatures of your fridges and keep a written record of them. This serves two purposes. If a fridge starts to fail, you will become aware of the temperature rise more quickly than if you do checks once a week.

Secondly, a written record could prove useful if the EHO has any queries, it shows you are serious about food temperature control.

The Four Hour Rule

If you remove chilled food from a refrigerator, you are allowed to display it above 8 degrees C for a maximum of four hours. Even though this is permitted, I wouldn't dream of exposing a sandwich to four hours of ambient temperature, and neither should you.

I have a feeling that this regulation may be amended in the future. Even when preparing sandwiches, your chilled ingredients such as cold meats should not be exposed for four hours.

In theory you could sell sandwiches from a non-refrigerated van using this rule, although if there were any complaints the onus would be on you to prove that you had complied with the law.

It's a good idea to buy a digital temperature probe that you can insert into a sample of your chilled products, as a periodic check up on the effectiveness of your fridge units. Even though there will probably be an internal or external gauge fitted to your fridge, it doesn't hurt to verify the temperature reading using a hand held probe.

Don't be a cheapskate like me and buy the lowest cost unbranded probe you can find, or will you run yourself ragged trying to figure out why your fridges never get cold enough. Buy a decent probe that actually indicates the correct temperature reading.

Hot Food

Food that is served hot has to be at a minimum of 63 degrees Celsius. That's the legal requirement. This rule applies to food warmers in your kitchen prep area and to the warmer in the van (if it has one fitted).

However, if you serve food that cold, you will lose your pie eating clientele very quickly – fortunately warmers tend to operate at around 80 degrees Celsius. Reheating food is permitted under the law, but I don't recommend it.

Preventing food contamination

Hazard Analysis Critical Control Point (HACCP)

Not nearly as complex as it sounds, but a very important part of the regulations. Basically, what it boils down to is that you have to analyse every part of your business and examine any areas that might lead to food contamination, or spoilage.

You have to draw up a plan of action to make sure that any potentially hazardous situations are avoided.

An example

You might store opened packets of bacon above the cheese slices in your fridge, there would be a risk of contamination if bacon fell onto the cheese. A simple solution would be to store meat products on the lower shelves, and cheeses above. If cheese crumbs fell onto raw bacon, it's not a health risk because it gets cooked before it is eaten.

The Five Points of a Hazard Analysis Plan

The current approach to drawing up a hazard analysis control sheet is based upon five principles.

1. Analysis of the potential causes of food contamination in a business.

There are three main sources of contamination that could occur. Bacterial growth, which could cause food poisoning. Contamination by foreign material such as plastic, glass or metal. Chemical contamination such as cleaning material or pest poisons.

2. Identification of the points in food production where hazards may occur.

Food, for example a sandwich, goes through many stages before it is finally prepared. Buying the supplies, storing them, mixing the ingredients etc, hazards could occur at any of the stages. You have to identify the hazard points.

3. Identifying which of the hazard points are critical.

You have already identified the hazard points in step two. Now you must decide which of those points are critical. Which of the food preparation steps could lead to contamination? A simple example might be preparing raw bacon on a surface, then immediately chopping onions, without first cleaning that surface.

4. Implementing measure to prevent the critical hazards and making sure that staff adheres to them.

You have to introduce measures for those critical points where contamination could occur and you have to introduce checks to make sure the measures are adhered to. In the example of the raw bacon contaminating the onion, you could introduce colour coded chopping boards so that vegetables and meats are never chopped on the same board.

To make sure the measure was adhered to, you would need to introduce a check, which could be a daily reminder, or random inspection.

5. Review your hazard analysis plan periodically.

It's no use drawing up your hazard analysis sheet then leaving it buried in your drawer. You have to make sure that the routines in place to prevent critical hazards developing are being followed, and are working. You may need to modify or update routines. With food, you can never be complacent about the potential hazards.

Dealing With the Environmental Health Officer

Public awareness of food related health problems and contamination has increased dramatically over the past ten years or so. Mad Cow disease, Bird Flu, Foot and Mouth, salmonella - just about everybody will have heard the horror stories. The authorities took note, and food hygiene became the in thing and it still is.

This cannot be seen as a bad thing; after all, the chief aim of increased regulation and control is a better quality of life for all of us. Unfortunately for those of us in the sandwich or catering industry, it does involve extra work and visits from the Environmental Health Officer.

Registering your business

You have to register with your local authority at least 30 days before you open. Hopefully you will have contacted them long before that, as suggested in the chapter on planning and fitting out your kitchen. The EHO can offer practical advice on your kitchen and equipment long before you are even ready to open. Points to note are:

- The EHO can visit, unannounced, and has the power to close your business if it is deemed necessary. The good news is that they are interested in helping you comply with the law; you are highly unlikely to find one who is overly officious or unpleasant.

- The EHO will be taking his guidance from the same book as you, 'The Industry Guide to Good Hygiene Practise' – makes communication much easier.

In the grand scheme of things, sandwich businesses are seen as less of a risk than other food outlets. Convince the EHO that you are doing your best to comply with the regulations and you will have fewer visits.

Nonetheless, a visit can still be a bit unsettling. They will quite often find something that needs to changed or improved, even if it is a small point. Make sure you know your food storage temperatures and can produce your hazard analysis control sheet.

Hygiene Training For Your Employees

You might not have any employees, not at first anyway, but if you do then training will be required. There are two levels of training that can be given to staff: informal in-house guidelines, and formal outside training.

In-house guidelines

Basic personal hygiene and any specific requirements you might have should be written down in your staff training manual. Some of the points will be relatively obvious even to the newest staff member. For example, insisting that hands are always washed thoroughly after visiting the toilet. You still have to detail it though.

It's no good stating that, 'good hygiene practise must be observed at all times', you need more precision than that. Typical considerations might be:

- Reporting any stomach bug, runny nose, sore throat or cuts.

- Always wash hands when returning from a rest break, or from anywhere outside the food preparation area.

- Not leaving dirty equipment such as knives or graters to accumulate.

- Disposing of waste ingredients, not leaving them in the food preparation area.

- Understanding the risks of cross contamination (by chopping raw bacon, then cheese on the same board without first cleaning it, for example)

- Always using a blue plaster for any cut (better visibility in case the plaster somehow dislodges and comes into contact with food ingredients).

Formal Training Courses

All staff members involved in the preparation of food must also undergo formal training.

There are currently three levels of training. Level one, which provides basic information for people new to the food industry, and is really an elementary introduction, and levels two and three which provide intermediate and advanced training.

Subjects covered in the Elementary Level One training Course.

The regulations demand that anyone involved in the production of food must be trained to level 1 within three months of employment, unless that person never handles unwrapped food.

The average course lasts between 6 and 7 hours, effectively one working day, although some offer a two day split course. The curriculum will include:

- Food hygiene

- Food poisoning
- Bacteriology
- Temperature control
- Contamination
- Hazard Analysis
- Personal hygiene
- Stock control and preservation
- Pest control
- Cleaning
- Legislation

The course is very straightforward, and not at all taxing, including the section on bacteriology.

Course Providers

Information on courses can be found online, if your local authority has a website, or from your EHO. The course cost is quite low and varies between £65- £75

The Van

The EHO are concerned mostly with where the food is prepared. As long as your van is clean and the temperature rules are observed, they are unlikely to cause you any bother.

Vigilance is all important

Good hygiene practise is essentially just a matter of applying common sense, but that is no reason to get complacent. Remember to maintain your HACCP; it's not just a formality, but a genuinely beneficial aid.

Lastly, it can be difficult in a busy environment to keep your eye on everything, but when it comes to food hygiene you have to make sure that you (and any staff) follow the rules at all times.

Chapter Twelve

General Issues

A lot of the general operational issues can only be finalised once you have been running for a while and have a feel for how the business is developing. Nevertheless, it's useful to sort out as much as you can before you start trading.

Setting Your Trading Hours

There will be a certain amount of experimenting before you can determine your best working hours – it will depend on the market you are targeting.

Generally, for office parks and general trading estates, you need to be on the road and ready to sell by about 10am. That is seen as the first tea-break for most workers and that is when people start eating. If you plan on selling earlier, then you are targeting the breakfast crowd – and if you can get that right, it can be very lucrative.

Most sandwich vans would continue selling until around 2.30pm. Any later than that and potential sales are pretty thin on the ground.

Of course, just because you finish selling mid afternoon, does not mean your working day is over. There will be plenty of other tasks to keep you busy, especially in the early days of the business – before you have established a set routine.

Keeping the Van Clean

I recommend washing the van at least every second day. You will be amazed how quickly the grime builds up. I am not talking a full valet here, just a daily wash to remove the worst of it. Once a week, give it a proper clean.

Taking Payment by Card and Cheque

The majority of your sales will be fairly modest and the customers can usually afford to pay in cash. An average order might consist of a sandwich, packet of crisps or a cookie and a cold drink. The buying public don't generally expect mobile vans to offer credit card payment options – although you might occasionally have to deal with a hopeful individual trying his/her luck.

Cards

Mobile card terminals do exist, so it's technically possible to offer card payment as an option. However, there are serious cost implications and I don't recommend you go down this route.

Up to three percent of the value of a sale is charged as commission, which is paid to the handling company. You could pass this charge on to the customer (by law you are entitled to) but that would be seen as penny pinching and customers would resent it.

In addition to this, you will have to pay the initial set up costs before you take a single card payment. This can run into hundreds of pounds. Finally, you have to wait for your money. It can take a month or longer before it enters your bank account.

Cheque

Some customers may want to pay by cheque; it's still a common form of payment. Only accept them in conjunction with a guarantee card, no other retailer in the land would consider otherwise, so why should you? I got caught once with a bounced cheque, but it didn't happen again. Now, I will only take a cheque with a valid guarantee card, even if it means losing a sale.

Running a Tab

Bit of a tricky one this. Some of your customers might want to, 'Buy now, pay later' – offering to settle up at the end of the week or on pay day. Naturally, it's best if you can avoid this situation completely.

You don't want to be bullied into agreeing, fearing lost sales if you don't, but at the same time, it might be an option for regular trusted customers.

I have always avoided it from day one. That way, the rule is in place and applies to everyone. Your situation might be a little different – for example if your competitors allow it, then you might want to consider it too.

Dealing with the float

Between £100 and £120 should be enough for your float. Break this down into a fair selection of notes and coins. Pay special attention to the number of £5 notes, they will be your fastest movers, so it pays to keep enough on hand.

A moneybag attached to your belt is the most common way to carry the float with you – it needs to be with you at all times, you cannot take the risk of leaving it in a tin on the front seat.

During the day, as your takings build up, you will need to siphon off the excess, otherwise your moneybag will become overloaded. Some vans have a hidden safe installed, which is perfect for storing the takings. Otherwise, earmark a hidden location in the van and periodically transfer the takings to it.

Don't transfer money to the secret location whilst you are busy at the stop – it needs to stay secret. Also, don't go rooting for change for the same reason.

Working out Your Banking Routine

Since most of your takings will be in cash, it follows that banking is going to play an important part in your routine. It's likely that you will bank several times a week. Don't always bank at the same time, taking the same route. You need to vary the routine in the interests of security. Also, don't use a distinctive carry bag; you must be as unobtrusive as possible.

You might be able to limit your trips to the bank, if you can work out a routine for paying local suppliers in cash. That's not always as easy as it sounds though. A lot of suppliers are geared towards card and cheque payments.

Coping With Price Changes

Inevitably there will be times when your prices have to change. On rare occasions there will be reductions, but more usually a supplier will raise their prices and you'll have to follow suit and pass the increases onto your customers.

Don't change suppliers for the sake of a few pence here and there, but if the rises are drastic and above inflation, then look into the reasons, and if necessary find alternative sources.

Unfortunately, you won't know when a supplier is going to alter their pricing structure and this can make it difficult to implement your own increases. If you use a dozen suppliers and they all raise prices at some point during the year, how will you respond? Raise your own prices a dozen times? Do nothing for fear of losing custom? Look for a new supplier base? There is no easy answer. One thing is certain; there is a constant gradual upward pressure on prices that will affect your profit unless you have a game plan.

The only realistic option is to pass on the increases to the end user, namely, your customers. If you don't, then your profit and possibly the viability of the business will be called into question.

Probably the best course of action is a once yearly increase, trying to take into account the expected supply cost changes for that year. It's not an exact science, more of a best guess situation.

Planning a Break

It's highly unlikely that you'll be considering any kind of holiday during your first year. That's not unusual, most business people think the same way - so much to do and so little time. By the second year of operation you ought to be planning a proper break.

There is a danger of believing that your business would collapse without you at the helm. That you can never take a break, and that holidays are for other people. This sort of mindset doesn't do anything for your health and is probably untrue as well.

If you took a week off, would your sandwich round really go to rack and ruin? Granted, there are certainly difficulties to sort out, but plan ahead and there is no reason you can't take a break the same as everyone else.

My holidays are always planned around Christmas because it's generally a quiet time. For several years running I have stopped completely over the festive season. There may be a small risk of losing customers with this strategy, but so far it's worked out fine.

Most businesses wind down over the Christmas period, so it's quite likely that your sandwich round could close for a while too. You will lose some takings, but that's a small price to pay for the luxury of a nice break at the end of the year.

Outside Factors Affecting Your Business

It's easy to forget about the outside world when you are busy with the daily issues concerning your business. Keeping customers happy, checking on suppliers, trying out new sandwiches, serving customers, it's all part of an average day.

Even when the working day is over, you'll have tasks to keep you busy (You weren't expecting to sort out the paperwork during work hours, were you?).

As the months pass and you establish a regular routine, you'll have more time to examine outside factors that could affect your business. You can't control or predict these factors or events, but you can be aware of them.

Food Scares

Ever since the BSE crisis was revealed to UK consumers a few years back, food safety has become a very delicate issue. The public has had to contend with BSE, the foot and mouth outbreak, the salmonella egg scandal, bird flu and Sudan1 contamination. Any of these events could affect your business negatively.

For example, an outbreak of bird flu (which predominantly affects imported poultry) could damage sales of chicken sandwiches. Every time BSE is in the news, meat sales suffer.

Whenever a food scare come along you have to try and negate the damage. If your sandwich sales are suffering because of bird flu fears, then use only British chicken, and broadcast the fact. The point is, you have to be aware of external happenings because they could affect your business, don't just ignore them. Generally, food scares pass into memory and people go back to buying all their old favourites again. You have to manage the situation as best you can in the meantime.

Bad Publicity

Recently, I watched a high profile TV documentary about the sandwich industry. It was an expose and it wasn't flattering. The producers chose to concentrate on two separate areas.

- The fat, sugar and salt contents of the ingredients.
- The hygiene standards that the sandwiches were prepared under.

They sampled sandwiches from a variety of high street chains and analysed the contents of each. Some sandwiches didn't do so well but others achieved a reasonable score on the health meter.

The second part of the program concerned an independent sandwich manufacturing company – subjected to undercover filming. The secret footage did not show the company in a good light. Without going into details, it's fair to say that the film showed some pretty horrific lapses in basic, common sense hygiene.

I doubt that anyone would've willingly eaten their sandwiches after seeing that program – I certainly wouldn't have.

Damage control

Bad publicity can do more damage than a food scare, because it calls into question the very idea that the public will always happily buy food from external sources.

The public are growing ever more concerned with issues such as health and hygiene. You can be sure that a segment of the public will never purchase anything from a mobile van because of programs like this.

You may have to counteract the negative image caused by others in the food industry. Unfortunately, every time there is a major case involving any kind of food establishment, everyone in the industry comes under suspicion – and that includes sandwich round operators.

Your only defence is to ensure you observe the hygiene rules and be ready to answer questions from a concerned buying public. If necessary, emphasize the cleanliness of your preparation area, maybe even have a few photos on your website.

Of course, if you buy someone else's sandwiches to re-sell, you have to trust them to maintain the correct standards.

The Weather and Local Developments

Within a few months of opening you will notice how the weather affects your sales. The local forecast takes on a new meaning when you know it can affect your livelihood.

Becoming an expert meteorologist is unnecessary; just note the forecast for a few days in advance. Sometimes, predicting sales is easy – everyone seems to like hot food even more in winter for example.

After you've been trading for a while, patterns will emerge that will help you to predict how the weather will affect your sales.

Local developments

Roadworks can play havoc with your daily takings. A major part of your time will be spent travelling, so you need to know if upcoming roadworks will impact your route. To be fair, you normally have plenty of warning, but there is very little you can do about it, other than plan an alternative route in advance. Otherwise you risk becoming traffic bound when you should already be at the next stop.

The Competition

Don't become complacent. Keep an eye on your competition. Have they changed their price structure recently? Or added unusual items to the menu? Are they experimenting with any new marketing ideas?

Keeping track of your rivals can be difficult, they are mobile vans after all, but its something you should try and do. Perhaps check their website (if they have one) for latest news and offers. Maybe chat to your own customers and try to pick up some pointers.

Keep up with Trends

Adopting a new trend or idea could give you an advantage over your opposition. A good source of news and ideas is *'Sandwich and Snack News'*, a periodical aimed at the sandwich industry. Take advantage of the internet, there are numerous sites dedicated to the sandwich and catering trades. Have a look at hot trends in other countries, again by searching the net. Also, know the difference between a trend and a fad; don't jump on the bandwagon before carefully weighing up the pros and cons of a new product.

Fads

New diets appear almost weekly, recommending certain foods, either natural or enhanced. Most of them die a death after a brief burst of publicity. It would be fair to describe these diets, and many of the associated food products, as fads. By all means take an interest in fads, but it pays to be aware of current and growing trends because that's how you will grow your business.

Employing a Driver

The majority of sandwich rounds tend to be run by owner operators. The person who owns the sandwich van also drives and serves from it. Naturally this gives the owner the most control over the daily takings.

However, if you do intend to hire a driver then there are a couple of things to be aware of.

Building up the round

A driver is employed to visit the businesses you have already acquired as customers. You cannot realistically expect the driver to go cold calling and do all the marketing for you – that is your job. If you rely on the driver to create the business for you, you probably won't build up much of a customer list – but you may end up losing the driver.

Once you have spent some time establishing the round, then you could consider employing a driver. This person would have to serve the customers as well. Employing two people would not be feasible.

Commission

The only way you can be sure that the driver will visit all of the customers is to provide an incentive. The most common way is by offering a commission on every sale that is made.

The costs

As well as the legalities of employing staff, there are significant costs involved too. When these are added to the wages and commission bill, it becomes apparent that only the busiest operators can afford to employ drivers.

Chapter Thirteen

Pre-Launch Day and Beyond

Your first trading day is fast approaching, perhaps less than a week away. The kitchen preparation area has been completed (assuming you are making your own sandwiches) and systems are in place to ensure the smooth running of the business.

Now is a good time to prepare a checklist to make sure you've covered everything. Your first few weeks of trading will fly by and you will be making adjustments to some aspect of the business virtually daily. Changes could be anything from altering suppliers, to dropping or changing a sandwich line – even altering prices.

Preparing a Pre-launch Checklist

Drawing up a list might help to iron out problems before they start. The checklist will be unique to your business, but points to consider would include:

- The menu must be ready, and anyone involved should be trained to confidently prepare sandwiches. Making them for friends or relatives is good practise for the real thing.

- The legalities of the business should be in order. Insurance policies for the van, buildings and content and public liability should be in place.

- You must have a good range of suppliers lined up – essential for the smooth running of the venture.
- Have printed menus available to hand out

- If possible get a website developed – doesn't have to be fancy or expensive, just informative.

Draw up a Contact List

If you need a plumber, vehicle technician, refrigeration engineer or electrician in a hurry, you don't want to start thumbing through the yellow pages. Prepare this list in advance and keep it handy

Announcing Your Presence

Marketing, in our context, is just a term used to describe the act of getting your business known. There are plenty of ways you can do this, without spending vast amounts of money. Some of the best advertising can be had for free, or at least very cheaply.

Fortunately, your customers will be from a relatively small geographical area. There won't be any need for expensive national or even county wide advertising.

The local newspaper

People are always curious about new food businesses. Most towns have a free newspaper delivered weekly. The editorial teams are constantly on the look out for interesting local developments. The opening of a new sandwich round, especially if it offers something a bit different, definitely qualifies.

Call the paper, let them know when you will be starting, mention any special offers. They will publish an article, usually with at least one photo, and tell the public all about you. This kind of free advertising is invaluable, and should never be overlooked.

You might find that the newspaper is happy to write an article, but on condition that you place an advertisement with them. Even so, the value of the editorial far exceeds the cost of placing an advert.

Target the local office parks and industrial estates

You will have already done your market research on these estates, just to establish that there is a market for your products. Now you should target them with printed matter.

Have a batch of brochures printed and do your best to get them distributed within the buildings. This is often easier said than done. You will probably have to drop your leaflets at reception, with no guarantee that they will be given out.

Naturally, it can be very frustrating if there are offices full of potential customers, but no way of reaching them. Your best way of solving this problem is to offer an incentive to the receptionist.

If the receptionist agrees to distribute your brochures, offer him/her free sandwiches for a week. That's a fair deal for both parties. You should have vouchers given out at the same time, offering price discounts, free cookies etc. Consider offering a loyalty card (after five purchases, you get a free sandwich, for example). You need people to try your van at least once, freebies or promotions are a good way of achieving that.

Cold calling

This involves phoning the businesses on the estates you plan to visit and asking if it would be okay to visit and drop off some menus. If they agree, you can use that opportunity to promote your sandwich round – just be sure to get the name of the person you spoke to.

Telephoning is a viable alternative to just appearing at the door, hoping to get in, but it does take a little practise before most people are comfortable with it.

Telephone technique

Few people enjoy receiving cold calls because most of the time it's just a sales pitch. Asking permission to drop off a few menus or brochures doesn't fall into the same category though. Most of the time, your call will meet with success.

A simple intro phone call might be something like this:

'Hello,
I wonder if you can help me. My name is Andrew Johnson and I have just started a new sandwich round in your area. Would it be ok to drop off a few menus?'

Keep it simple and concise – receptionists don't have time to listen to long speeches.

Get a website

A website gives you the chance to explain who you are and what you do. It can be used to inform customers of the latest offers as well as provide an online menu. A website does not have to cost the earth, those days are long gone.

A simple two or three page site can be had for less than £150. There are plenty of website companies to choose from. Search online and you will find literally thousands.

If you would like a website that you can update yourself, then you need a content management system (CMS). There are several totally free ones available for your use. A good example is the Joomla CMS (www.joomla.org). Count on spending a day learning how to add content and create articles – you don't need technical ability for this.

Installing Joomla can be a little tricky, if you have never dealt with a website before, but a web company could have it up and running in its basic useable form within an hour – so they shouldn't charge much for that.

Surviving the First Day

There is a lot to learn about dealing with the general public. Often someone will query something and you won't have a ready answer. A typical example would be something like this.

Customer, in a loud accusing voice, just to make sure the whole business park hears. "Your sandwiches are expensive, Joe's van is much cheaper, charging a bit much aren't you then?"

You, caught off guard and trying not to sound like a greedy opportunist "Well, er, ingredients cost and rent and er, um "

That's how I responded when faced with that situation for the first time. I was simply caught off guard. It can be embarrassing, especially as you know that Joe's sandwiches are a bit cheaper because they are filled with lower quality ingredients.

How to answer the belligerent customer? Give him a full cost structure breakdown? Tell him that Joe sells inferior sandwiches, so obviously yours will cost more? Start an argument to make sure you get your point across? Shrug your shoulders?

Diplomacy

Don't start a long conversation on the matter and don't get annoyed. Keep your response simple, polite and short. My standard refrain is. "Well we do our best to keep prices down, but we only use the very best ingredients and sometimes that costs a bit more". It's a true answer and can be delivered confidently because of that.

You might have this conversation in the first hour of your first day, or it might not happen for a week. Rest assured though, it will happen. You'll probably be rattled on other occasions as well. Always answer calmly without panicking or becoming annoyed. It gets easier once you have been trading for a while. You gain experience and confidence when dealing with the public.

The do's and don'ts on Your First Trading Day

Your first day is about introducing your business to the world; you need to make the best impression possible in every way. Little things will go wrong, no matter how well you plan. But as long as you have prepared well and done your research, you can avoid the most common problems.

Don't panic if you can't satisfy everybody

With the best will in the world, no matter how good your menu is, somebody is going to request something you don't keep. If several people make the same request, then investigate further, perhaps it's something you should be offering. Otherwise just accept that you cannot cater to every segment of the sandwich market.

Don't raise your voice

When you get busy, you might start to panic, thinking that it's taking too long to serve each customer, that the queue at the van is too long. Remember it's your first day. You will get faster at your job as time goes by. Never raise your voice or shout at anyone, customers will find it amateurish. Basil Fawlty might be fine on TV, but not in real life.

Make sure you order enough supplies

Over order if necessary, your first day will be eventful enough without the worry of ingredient shortages. Waste is a fact of life in the sandwich business, after a while you will get it down to sensible levels. But for the first few days on the road, you don't want to be worrying about running short on supplies.

Don't let your frustrations show

Some customers will dawdle, taking ages over every decision. Unfortunately that is all part of the game. It won't help getting ratty with them. You just have to grin and bear it.

Be prepared to make changes

Be prepared to make changes on opening day if it becomes blatantly obvious that something isn't working. This refers to any area of the business.

Don't get defensive if customers are critical

If the criticism is genuinely useful, then note it down, otherwise smile and grit your teeth. Don't engage with argumentative people, it can ruin your day and leave a bad impression on other customers.

Don't make up stories

Informed customers often ask detailed questions about specific ingredients - then look at you expectantly for an answer. If you have the information to hand, then all well and good. If not, then don't be tempted to create an answer, it's seldom a good idea. Rather admit that you don't know, but will find out.

Be friendly

Be nice to your customers. A cheerful friendly attitude is vital. You will be under a lot of pressure on opening day. A sullen stressed out sandwich round operator won't go down well with your customers.

Managing the occasional little crisis

It is your duty to remain calm and collected during your first day and beyond. You can't afford to panic or get stressed out in front of customers. Problems will certainly arise, right from the first day, but you have to manage them.

You can't let every little issue affect you as though it were a full blown crisis; otherwise you'll be worn out in no time. Even after one days trading, you will see areas of your operation that need changing or improving.

There will be a process of fine tuning for at least the first month. After that, a pattern of stability will emerge, and going to work will become less stressful.

After the First Few Weeks

You have to stand back and look at the business objectively. It's up to you to analyse how well things are going and what changes may need to be made.

Changes could be as minor as dropping an unpopular sandwich from the menu, to changing the route. It's not just internal procedures that must be analyzed. How do your customers see the business? From their viewpoint you have to find out:

- Do customers enjoy buying from you?

- Are customers being served quickly enough?

- Is the quality of the food satisfactory? Have you had any complaints? - if so, how are you going to resolve them?

- Are you building up a stream of regulars? Or do people come once and not again?

- Are your prices competitive? You don't need to be the cheapest; your sandwiches may cost more, but soft drinks /crisps and other 'ordinary things' should cost no more than your competitors.

Examine the issues

An examination of these issues might reveal that changes are needed to your business. It can be tempting to, 'bury your head in the sand', to avoid making a severe change or hard decision. Unfortunately this doesn't solve the problem. If anything it aggravates it.

You may need to drop suppliers, alter your prices (either higher or lower) and perhaps even consider getting some help, if you are feeling the strain.

The process of analysing your business objectively is an ongoing one, but is especially important during the early days. Even though you must always be alert and keep your eye on the ball, there will come a time when the business settles into a regular stable routine. This can take a few months, so don't expect to have ironed out all the little difficulties and problem areas in the first week.

Chapter Fourteen

Expanding the Business

Cutting costs can increase your turnover and potentially your profit, but there is a limit to the savings that you can make. Become overly penny pinching and the efficiency of the business could suffer.

There is also a limit to the number of people you can realistically expect to serve from the van. You will eventually reach a sales limit and to substantially increase your income will mean expanding the business somehow – perhaps venturing into other food related areas such as catering.

Once you have one van on the go, it can be tempting to assume that the next step should be getting another and building up a small fleet. It seems to make sense on many levels. More income, more buying power with suppliers, a chance to start your empire. However, unless you approach the idea cautiously, the result will be a doubling or tripling of your workload, without much financial benefit.

Do you really want the added hassle?

Before you commit to any expansion, you need to ask yourself if you really want to. It's going to mean taking risks and dealing with a lot of uncertainty, which is meat and drink to an entrepreneur, but is that why you started out in the first place?

If you wanted a fleet of vans all along, then fine, carry on as planned. But if your original ambition was to start a sandwich round to provide a good income for your family, and you are happy with that, then leave empire building to the budding tycoons. Managing one van, with you there every day, is one thing. Starting and running a fleet, with all the negotiating and organising involved, is another. Different skill sets are required, the primary one being the ability to delegate.

That said, it's worth noting that some operators do take the concept further. I know of at least one independent in the North of England who has a fleet of fifteen vans. This is obviously a totally different league when compared to starting one sandwich round with one van.

The question is, are you prepared to risk everything you already have, to pursue the dream of a business empire? If the answer to this question is no, then planning a fleet of vans, with multiple sandwich rounds, is probably not the best way forward for you.

Alternatives to Fleet Building

If you want to increase your turnover, but are not keen on buying more vans, there are quite a few options open to you. Some will involve a small investment, others make use of the assets you already have.

Supplying Sandwiches on a Wholesale Basis

Supplying other outlets with your sandwiches is a very appealing idea, since it's just a continuation of what you already doing, namely, producing sandwiches.

Obvious targets are local shops and cafes who might like to carry a range of fresh sandwiches, but aren't geared up for production. Don't ignore petrol station forecourt shops. Next time you fill up with fuel, have a look at the selection. A lot of these shops sell sandwiches made by small local companies.

In theory you could even approach local supermarkets and offer them your product range. In practise though, you might find the profit margin too small and the payment period too long, in some cases getting your money could take 90 days.

Wholesaling your sandwich products to other shops is not something you can tackle half heartedly; you need to be fully geared up for it. Some of the points to consider are:

- To deliver in any appreciable quantity, would need a refrigerated vehicle. Not an expensive mobile food van, just a standard fridge van. Used ones can be had for about £1500.

- Any food products you supply to an outlet must be labelled according to the Quantitative Ingredient declarations regulations (QUID), with nutritional details and a complete breakdown of the ingredient percentages.

- You might have to offer sale or return, depending on the competition in your area, and this has to be factored into your price.

- You will have to supply your sandwiches fully sealed, not in standard clear hinged wedges. This will mean investing in a heat sealer. Don't buy a second hand heat sealer unless you can examine the hot plate, they are often worn out or have 'hot spots' that make sealing difficult. A new machine would cost about £600.

There is no doubt that supplying sandwiches wholesale could lead to a profitable business that may outstrip your original sandwich round, as long as you do your market research to gauge demand before proceeding.

Setting up a Specialised Food Delivery Service

At the most basic level, customers phone their orders through, you prepare that order and deliver at a specified time. The service is normally cash on delivery. This simple setup is used effectively by plenty of businesses. As with any other venture, the key is organisation.

Your business is already suited to offering an ordering service, you just need to implement a system that is easy to use and understand. Will you be delivering at set times? Or as soon as a customers order is ready? Will you be offering hot food, such as toasties, or just cold sandwiches?

The more flexible you are, the more sales you can expect, but that has to be balanced against the increased workload.

Online Ordering – a Potential Goldmine

Ordering your lunch over the internet seems a little over the top – a bit like using technology for the sake of it. Up until recently I would have described this as a fad, now I am not so sure. A growing number of businesses are offering an online ordering facility, some systems are simple but others are more complex.

The basics

At the simplest level, you would log onto a website, browse the food menu, then send an email with your choices and delivery details. Your order would be delivered at a set time and payment made. It takes a few minutes to type the email, but that's the only effort involved.

More advanced

A more advanced website would have the food menu displayed, and you fill in a form online (usually by ticking checkboxes to make your selection). When ready you click the send button and the order is processed. Your order arrives and you pay for it. This is even easier than sending an email; you complete your order with a few clicks of the mouse.

Online Shop

The most advanced websites allow you to browse the online food menu, fill in an online form, and then pay for the order by credit card. By registering as a regular user, you click one button to pay, instead of entering your card details every day.

When you consider how many office workers have access to computers, but very little time for lunch, the appeal of online ordering becomes clear. No messing around trying to place a phone order, no rushing out to grab a quick bite on the run. No panicking because the sandwich van just drove off. As long as the ordering and payment procedure is simple to use and reliable, anyone specialising in this field could be onto a goldmine

A few years ago, it would have cost a fortune to set up an online shop like this. Nowadays, there are free website packages available and plenty of small business owners make use of them. Some good examples would be:

- OsCommerce – (http://www.oscommerce.com)

- Zencart – (http://www.zen-cart.com)

- Magento – (http://www.magentocommerce.com)

Allowing people to pay online by card encourages higher value purchases. Even during lean periods when cash is tight (like just after Christmas) people still have access to plastic.

There are costs involved in the initial setup when you want to take credit card payments, but if you are developing an online shop, then card payment is realistically the best option.

Specialising in Home Baked Confectionaries

If you have the space and the time, manufacturing your own range of biscuits, cakes or cookies could be a wise move. Not only would you sell the products from your own van, but possibly to other outlets as well. You would need to purchase a commercial grade mixer which unfortunately is not cheap.

A few years ago I investigated the possibility of manufacturing biscuits and cookies for sale to other shops. The market research showed that the idea was feasible. The equipment requirements were quite modest. A dough mixer was needed as well as a cookie / biscuit press.

The mixer was priced at £1700 for a new model, or about £380 for a used one (you have to buy strong commercial grade quality) and the cookie press was a manually operated Kook-E-King. The press was a delightful bit of kit. You put dough into a hopper, turned a handle, and rows of cookies were pressed out. Great fun.

Eventually the project was shelved, purely because of space limitations. We simply didn't have the room. I remain convinced that the home baked cookie / biscuit market is under catered for in the UK. It could prove a profitable niche for anyone with enough room to set it up.

Outside Catering

Offering a catering service could be a logical step. Learning what to offer and how to present it would take some practise, but it's certainly within your capability. If you make your own sandwiches, then you already have a suitable kitchen preparation area.

Search for caterers online and you will find loads of websites, many with menus, prices and descriptions of what they do. Mine this data and before long you would have a pretty good idea of what to charge per head in your area, as well as what to offer and in what quantities.

It would be wise to have a separate set menu for the catering side of things and not deviate from it to do one off specials. That kind of temptation can lead to all sorts of problems and foul ups.

What if special ingredients are needed? What if you forget to order them? Quite rapidly that cushy little one off order could turn into a loss making nightmare.

Delayed payment

One disadvantage is that you won't be paid in cash. You'll probably have to wait until the end of the month before the client company pays you.

No business is likely to pay you out of petty cash for a few platters of sandwiches. It's just something you have plan for and deal with.

Unfortunately it's easy to lose track of who has paid and who hasn't. You will need an invoicing system in place; otherwise you could find yourself losing out financially.

Catering for non corporate clients

The most obvious market here is wedding receptions. The main difference between a business function and a wedding is likely to be the number of people being catered for. A typical corporate meeting is a relatively small scale affair, perhaps 2 or 3 platters of assorted sandwiches. A wedding is a different ball game. Catering for big events takes a lot of planning and you could easily come unstuck unless you are highly organised.

Imagination is the key

The only real limit to how far you take things is your imagination. Whichever road you take, don't work yourself into an early grave, or be a martyr to the business and never take a holiday. Every now and then, stand back, relax and take a breather. Remember that the business is only one aspect of your life, make time to enjoy the rest of it.

Index

Lightning Source UK Ltd.
Milton Keynes UK
UKOW02f1647240814

237434UK00001B/53/P